HOW TO BE A

Smart

WOMAN IN
STEM

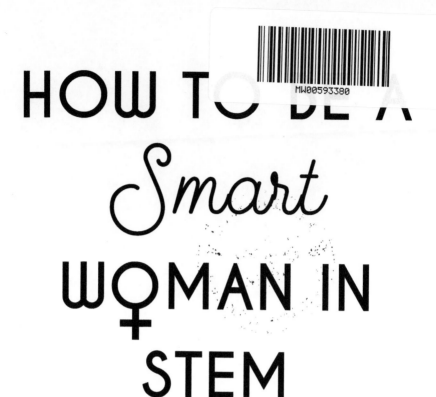

#SCIENCE #TECHNOLOGY
#ENGINEERING #MATH

Gabriela Mueller Mendoza

HOW TO BE A
Smart
WOMAN IN
STEM

Gabriela Mueller Mendoza

How to be a Smart Woman in STEM

First published in 2019 by

Panoma Press Ltd
48 St Vincent Drive, St Albans, Herts, AL1 5SJ, UK
info@panomapress.com
www.panomapress.com

Book layout by Neil Coe.

Printed on acid-free paper from managed forests.

ISBN 978-1-784521-53-0

The right of Gabriela Mueller Mendoza to be identified as the author of this work has been asserted in accordance with sections 77 and 78 of the Copyright, Designs and Patents Act 1988.

A CIP catalogue record for this book is available from the British Library.

Printed in Great Britain by TJ International Ltd.

For all the strong smart women who want to improve the world

and for Daniel, Leonardo, Emilio and my Mama who bravely walk in mine.

Testimonials

"A must read for women in STEM. You can be an expert in science and tech but without communications tactics it's hard to get what you want in tech. Spot on!"

Yi Jia Lim, Senior Leader in Cybersecurity, Singapore

"This book is a great tequila-shot of practical tools and advice, eye-opening and support for women in science and technology."

Emi Nagoshi, Associate Professor in Neuroscience, University of Geneva

"Women in STEM can gain so many practical tips in only one book. I really loved it."

Jeanette Teles, Global OpEx & CI Leader at ABB

"My new Swiss Army knife to get more funding, influencing my boss and peers!"

Beatrice Barra, Artificial Intelligence Specialist, Open AI Analytics, Brazil

"Very simple yet powerful toolset to reflect, stand up and thrive."

Begoña Chorén, Technology User Experience Strategist, Spain

Acknowledgements

As I travel the world, and especially over the past seven years, I have always kept two books in my handbag – one to read, and one to write in. I finally decided to write this one down. As it turns out, writing a book is harder than I thought and more rewarding than I ever imagined.

None of this would have been possible without my best friend, *corazón*, soulmate, Daniel. Thanks for your constant encouragement, love and believing in me. For taking leaps of faith in the past as my partner in crime and for keeping your cool when I lose mine.

To my mother, my loving *maestra*, my rock. Your love and strength are my compass. In memory of my beloved father. You both taught me that after falling, one gets up, dusts off and keeps playing. To my beloved sons, Leonardo and Emilio, my sunshine and moonlight, for showing me everything is possible. For your unconditional support, even if this meant missing handball matches at times or Sunday brunches. Thanks *mis amores*, for being just the way you are. I will always love you.

Thanks to my sisters, Lucy and Pao, for your love and always being there for me, no matter what and when. Natasha Lozano de Swaan, my friend, my sister, coach, mentor, thanks for the inspiration, the miles travelled together, the laughter, the tears and high fives.

Courageous leaders make this a better world and empower others to lead. Thank you to everyone who strives to make others grow. I was empowered at some point by their advice or example, all the way from the classroom to the boardroom. To everyone who I have had the opportunity to lead, be led by or witness their leadership, I say thank you for being the inspiration for *How to be a Smart Woman in STEM*.

Gratitude to my tribe, the relentless supporting circle of powerhouse women who challenge me to show up and be brave: Paola Brunnetta, Maya Burkhard, Elin Jusélius, Julie Fuhrmann, Valentina Locatelli, Verena Bender, Rebeca Olvera and Brenda Peregrina. And special thanks to Begoña Jiménez, Lucía Mathis, Gabriela Tejada, Emi Nagoshi, Jeanette Teles, Gloria Teo, Melanie Strauch and Eva Parth dos Santos for the inspiration, support and insightful expert input. To my wholehearted friends and family: Dirk Haseloff, Clara Jasso, Virginia Cerda, Raul Isunza, Yanira Schmid, Maria Petris and Elizabeth Schlumpf. Inspiration comes in all sizes and ages. I also want to remember all the children in my life and especially all the girls who I hope one day decide to discover the beauty in any STEM field: Sara, Fernando, Lucía Sofía, Gabriel, Citlali, Norma and mighty Emma.

Without the adventurous, exciting and insightful experiences around the world and my numerous teams, this book would not exist.

Thanks to my book coach, Mindy Gibbins-Klein, you were a great co-pilot, always energetic and keeping me focused. To my publisher's team for your talent and patience.

Thanks to Kim Molyneaux and the Panoma team for their editing work and advice and to Gabriel Jaun for your talent.

Gratitude to my inspiring friends and co-facilitators worldwide, for the incredible adventures in all five continents: Thomas Gelmi, Amy Carroll and Fabien Smadja. In every country that I have had the fortune to visit and work in, there is always a small group of supporting leaders on-site who make things happen. Too many to name you all – you are the engine of the change, empowering women from the grassroots all the way to senior leadership, such as Dominique Niyonizigiye, Silvia Gonzalez Pinto, Akiko Guevara and Nicole Hoevertsz to name a few. Thanks to all of you for your wholehearted support, you are all true leaders.

Special thanks to leaders and role models whose path I have had the chance to experience closely and who deeply inspire me: Anita L DeFrantz, Marisol Casado, Prof. Dr. Gudrun Doll-Tepper, Ian Roberts, Peter Bachmann, Tshering Zam and Beatrice Conde-Petit. The inspiring work of Gerd Leonhard, Simona Scarpaleggia, Dr. Thomas Bach, Brian Lewis, Ms Phumzile Mlambo-Ngcuka, Professor Yuval Noah Harari, Professor Klaus Schwab, Halla Tómasdóttir, Michael Kimmel and Alkistis Petropaki.

I would especially like to thank all the women and men in STEM fields whose stories and lessons I have had the chance to witness and collect as part of my coaching work throughout 17 years. From professors, professionals in academia, to former bosses. From peers, coachees, mentors, teachers, business owners, managers, corporate leaders, scientists, engineers, to mathematicians and researchers. Thank you.

Finally, a big thank you to **everyone** who ever said anything positive to me or taught me something. I heard it all, I kept it and it made a difference.

To all of you, *gracias.*

Contents

Acknowledgements 7

Before you read this book... 11

1. What got us here, won't get us there 25

2. No change no gain...33

3. Do's – your new Swiss Army knife 4.0..................... 43

4. Don'ts and things that can sabotage
   your success 77

5. Great things never came from comfort
   zones – take risks 87

6. Find your tribe and stick to it............................. 105

7. Politics is a game – learn the rules and
   test their elasticity 111

8. Recognise people's styles – persuade and
   reduce conflict.. 125

9. Get anyone to say yes – convince using the
   M&M Matrix 135

10. Negotiate like a pro – have big ambitions.............. 153

11. Women supporting women, assertiveness and
    hardcore tactics.. 165

12. Bad bosses, Queen Bees and great bosses.............. 181

13. Life hacks for working STEM mums – rockstars! .. 201

14. Advanced strategies for women in power
    and on boards.. 213

Conclusions 224

Notes and references 227

About the author.. 233

Before you read this book

Let's be future ready

You are here! You have decided to invest in you. You are about to find out how you can have more of what you want, more often and with less trouble! You will find out how to have the impact you want to have in this world. This book contains tools and strategies that will power up your career and your chances to make the changes you want to bring to the world. Use them to achieve your boldest goals as a smart woman in science, tech, engineering, math, business and all those fantastic fields that are relevant today and will be even more in the future. You are reading this book because you are one of the courageous minds involved in creating solutions for today and tomorrow.

I wish I had known most of the stuff in this book when I was in my early 20s when I worked as a new technology specialist in a large blue-chip company. Oh, did I make mistakes? You bet. Now 20 plus years later, I still haven't figured it all out yet – nobody has – though the good news is that now I can share many strategies that do work. I want you to have them, so I'll include stories, anecdotes, models and techniques that are easy to use and that stick in your mind like glue. Warning: side effects of using these strategies may well cause tremendous success in achieving your goals!

We've all had our 'Aha' moments in life. Epiphanies that give us either enlightenment and clarity or moments of sudden insight. When was the last time *you* experienced an Aha moment? This book came to be after several Aha moments that gave me insights, which I am ready to share with you. I believe the future of humankind is one that includes all of its potential at all levels.

Before we start, let's break the ice. I am from Mexico City. No small town. More than 20 million people in a buzzing, fast-rhythm city. In one of the largest cities on Earth, I learned to be quick, practical, pragmatic and street smart. These skills have helped me navigate all five continents.

My most inspiring souls in life are my two sons, and I admit, my No. 1 fan is my husband. Our home has been close to Bern, Switzerland for more than two decades. My enduring passion for making this a better world comes with my DNA as a relentless Mexican woman. My ancestors include inspiring, caring and brave women, like my mother, who taught me how to dance with fear instead of letting it run the show. I soon learned to go for my boldest goals, not without fear, but despite it, with courage. I haven't figured it all out, of course. The insights and recommendations in this book are things I know can work for you in STEM fields, when you decide to put them into practice.

Chica is a word I'll use throughout the book. It comes from my mother tongue, Spanish. I will use it to describe a powerful, smart woman with a good vibe, someone like you.

One of my recent 'Aha' moments was in Davos, Switzerland. Switzerland is home to some of the global events where leaders from around the world come and discuss the state of the world at the World Economic Forum. Their gender gap report shows that at the current rate of progress, the global gender gap will take 100 years to close. And in the workplace, the current gender gap will not be closed for 217 years at this pace. Wow! It's clear if we want to accelerate this change, we can all do more and must do more to get there. I want to propel the pace of this process and one of my contributions is this book.

I've been working as a coach and motivational speaker worldwide. My mission has always been to empower women to leap and lead. For the past two decades, I've dedicated my coaching work to empower women and help them advance. I started as a tech woman in my early 20s in technology, and went on to become a consultant in information technology. I've remained fascinated by technological advancements all my life and for what we can achieve for humankind through innovation.

Be courageous when attempting to change and implementing the tips in this book. It's not about major changes, it's about little steps which have a significant impact. First, use them in non-stressful situations where you feel more robust, rather than in larger endeavours. It will pay off, trust me.

My work and mission as a coach has taken me to over 80 countries. I've been writing notes, details and paragraphs for this book in some of the most amazing and inspiring places on Earth. I've written on notebooks, napkins and my computer, while drinking coffee in an old café in Bogotá, or sitting on a bench at the Louvre Museum, or enjoying a stroll in ancient Jerusalem. Sometimes in airport lounges, on planes, while taking a walk in the woods or riding busy trains, while enjoying a sunset on a beach in beautiful Costa Rica or in my quiet office close to Bern, Switzerland. I often looked out on the majestic Alps as I chose the golden nuggets, the ideas that can empower someone like you to advance and create the future solutions we all need.

Now I'd like to suggest you read this book with an open mind and heart. Hold your judgment about some of the strategies I will recommend. Stay open and curious. Use them, try them out several times, and only then decide what you'll keep in your toolbox.

Now, buckle up. Start filling your toolbox with kick-ass strategies that you can pull out anytime, everywhere, and apply anywhere you want to create an impact. Ready, steady, go!

The good, the bad and the ugly

We live in the most exciting time in history. Think about this: there is less poverty today than ever before. War isn't as common as it once was, in spite of what seems to dominate news broadcasts. In addition, diseases are in decline. My friend, a century ago we would not have lived to see 50! Humans are living longer and more fulfilling lives today.

Happiness is on the rise in the majority of countries around the world. The average surveyed person is now happier than a decade ago. With poverty, war, disease and violence all on the decline across the globe, there are many good reasons to be happy. Yes! It's a great time to be alive on this planet, and every breath is a gift.

Today, thanks to the power of the internet and connectivity, we are all aware of what's going on in a matter of seconds.

The stakes are high and as women in STEM fields, it is time to step up and take the decision-making positions that give access to the power to lead, have a say, create, innovate and thrive.

The 4th Industrial Revolution or 4IR is here. While the first three revolutions left us with tremendous advances, this new 4IR is modifying not only what, but how we do things. It will fundamentally change us, as humankind. I believe it's essential that female brains and feminine power are behind the wheel of this vehicle of change as well, driving these unique developments.

The bad and the ugly elements in these unique times are also global socio-political phenomena. In recent years, new nationalists came to power and rule some of the most influential countries today. The last few years have been the warmest on record. We've seen extraordinary, devastating hurricanes and natural disasters happen throughout the world. Yes, these are unique times.

The lack of women in key fields can increase the chance of creating a future that lacks inclusion, diversity of thinking and sustainability. This could bring about tremendous inequality in the world, and ultimately a world that only uses 50% of its population's potential.

I strive at creating the other possibility, a world in which women and men thrive together. For that to happen, we all have a role to play and something to contribute.

The good news is that the sense of urgency in which many leading organisations are addressing this issue is quick and clear. There is a realisation that will take a multidisciplinary effort to find new solutions and policies to ensure an inclusive talent pool. This potential includes women who are educated, recruited and promoted in a fair and wise manner.

Disclaimers

Some names and identifying details have been changed to protect the privacy of individuals. This book is not intended as a substitute for the medical advice of physicians or financial advisors. Following the advice in this book could potentially get you the results you wish in your career and life. On the other hand, depending on how and when you apply them, the outcomes will also be determined by the combination of external factors and other stakeholders' views and actions. I encourage you to recognise you've got more power to influence your results than you ever thought you had.

How to be a Smart Woman in STEM is not an academic paper or curriculum. It's a collection of strategies, anecdotes and tools to encourage the thriving path of women in science, technology, engineering and math. It also aims at raising the level or awareness and sense of urgency for the inclusion of more women in light of the current situation in these fields worldwide.

No magic trick will change your life or career for the better. It is only through your consistent and persistent practice of the tactics and methods shown in this book that you are closer to achieving your goals. The information contained within this book is strictly for educational purposes and intended as career advice.

Although some of the statistics of the presence of women in STEM fields are not encouraging, I intend to shine a light on to issues we can change. Aspects we can all influence and be proactive about. I am not naïve or pessimistic. I want to keep a proactive view and dynamic conversation that moves things forward, though without knowing the present situation there is little we can do about it.

Now that we've cleared that up let's get on discovering how powerful you can be when you are determined to get what you want sustainably and genuinely.

Setting the stage – women in STEM

Let's take a look at what the current situation looks like so we can wisely build the future.

At least half of the world workforce is made up of women. More women gain college and graduate degrees than men. And let's face it, women represent the largest single economic force in the world. Yet the gender gap in key areas of our societies persists, from politics to education to sports, to STEM fields. This phenomenon is more of a significant problem in STEM fields than in other professions, particularly in high-end, science and math-intensive fields, and definitely in computer science.

Although girls outperform boys in the majority of STEM subjects at entry level, the number of young female students who choose to study STEM falls significantly behind the percentage of men. In many advanced European countries, less than 10% of engineers are women.

So where does it start? Although we now know that the love for science usually happens before the age of 10, we see that over 60% of girls between 11 and 15 years of age believe STEM areas are just for boys. Such inaccurate perceptions hold girls back from considering a future in the technology industry. This fuels the negative perception by the population and talent in the other half of the world. It shows when we see how engineering products and services are not always sustainable and inclusive.

One of the fastest ways an organisation loses competitiveness and its advantage is by missing the chance that diversity offers. In a nutshell, the benefits of diverse teams are: better financial results, a positive impact on the bottom line, better return on investment, better return on sales, more employee engagement, more talent retention, better customer satisfaction and better equity. It's a no-brainer, you may think. It is. Gender diverse teams outperform the competition. Every time.

Despacito is a famous Latin song which means 'slowly'. That's how this development has progressed so far. Today there's more awareness, there are a few effective campaigns, and a few governments putting in effort to act in a more visionary way. But it's still too slow.

The good news is that there are many medium- and large-sized companies that already get it! You don't have to reinvent the wheel. There are key things that a workplace can do to retain valuable female talent in engineering and other science-related areas. Here are some: create a collaborative environment with policies that elicit flexibility and don't measure performance through face time. Offer leadership development, mentoring and networking for women. These factors can reap benefits by retaining women. And yes, retaining women in engineering is key for what's coming.

Me and my path in tech

I too started in technology. You see, between the 80s and 90s, thanks to booming demand, the number of women like myself pursuing studies in computer science continued to increase. At some point it reached 37% – twice what it is today. Then it began to plunge.

In Mexico City, my hometown, I remember being part of university study groups and work teams formed by at least 40-50% women in technology. In my early 20s I became an IBM employee for most of my computer science experience in Latin America and then Europe. Therefore, I can now appreciate the changes of today in this industry.

Mid-senior management teams were mostly male though. At first, I was involved in mid and mainframe computer platforms. Later, I got into Optical Character Recognition technology or OCR, helping financial institutions automate processes in Latin America. Afterwards I moved into IT consulting and I was based in Europe. I met some of my greatest mentors in tech. Men and women whose advice and friendship even today help me navigate other environments, now as a professional coach.

The tech world is a competitive one. I personally had an overall positive experience as a woman in tech. I have thrived under supportive peers and invested mentors. Whenever I experienced sexist comments or condescension, I didn't let those get under my skin. I was busy trying to get my stuff done, learning the new thing, looking for the next challenge. That's my nature. I know positive experiences can often get lost when only negative ones are highlighted.

After some years in tech jobs, after travelling the world and later becoming a mum, I decided to follow my true passion: empowering people in organisations that I care about, so they get better results and thrive. I got certified as a professional coach in London. I brought my set of transferable skills into coaching, training and even speaking.

For the past 17 years I've coached professionals in tech, sciences, academia, sports and business. Today, as a coach I closely work with technology companies and engineering partners that power up solutions to make this world a better place.

I continue to apply the advice of one of my mentors: comfort zone and growth don't go hand in hand. Leave the first to get the second one. I recommend it to you as you read this book.

Women running startups

Today, in technology, biotech, IT and other scientific fields, we see more women than ever starting their own company. Despite many barriers, the gender gap in computer science, all-male funding teams at venture capitals, and in many cases hostile workplaces, these women have found other means to challenge gender inequality. If you are a female entrepreneur, in this book you will also find strategies that will negotiate you better deals, more investors and form better teams.

Women can also lead startups and organisations that disrupt and create new market spaces, that defy older models and innovate. The percentage of venture-backed startups with at least one female founder is 17%. Lately there are increasing efforts to make diversity front-and-centre in the minds of many. Last year, startups led by all-women teams received about 2.2% of the total pot invested by venture capitalists. That will change because the latest studies found that startups with female founders tend to grow faster and get better results than those lacking women.

If you are one of them, welcome! You will find tactics and techniques to negotiate better deals, to pitch your ideas effectively and to get more support, more buy-in and reduce resistance.

Women in science

Interestingly the majority of students studying medical degrees in Europe are women. More than two-thirds of veterinary science students are female. Other preferred areas are ophthalmic, anatomy and pathology, and forensic studies.

Unconscious bias during the recruiting and selection process is a reality. There's a strong bias or prejudice against female applicants for grants and other positions, as they are often perceived to be less competent in selection processes. Experiments involving applicants who remove their names and personal information on the application form have proven that they are rated differently from when they go through the process revealing their female names.

Many organisations and institutions have put in place programmes to incentivise the presence of female scientists in many areas. Those efforts have yet to generate good results at large, though are a welcome start. All stakeholders have a role to play to change the situation and stop having women disproportionately represented and disadvantaged in scientific careers, compared to men.

Women in technology

Currently only 24% and an even lower percentage of women in technology is predicted by 2024 if nothing is done about it. Tech giants are lacking women. Many of the usual suspects, large companies in the world such as Google, Facebook and many global brands pride themselves on having that number of female employees. In fact, only around 16% of those women actually have jobs in tech within those giants. The European Union's average of women in tech is 16.7%.

Want to find good jobs? IT and computing are the fields where the jobs are — and where they will be in the future. Despite that fact, less than one in five computer science graduates are women. Even though tech jobs are in the fastest growing sector in the modern world, it's where we see the biggest drop off for young women too.

There is a clear disconnect between the need in the computer science industry and the efforts to inspire girls to choose technology in school. If you are in the position to influence any young girl or woman in your life, it is well worth reflecting and reversing this trend. You can have a substantial impact.

Businesses can increase innovation by having more women in their tech teams, in fact an increase of over 40% of business results. Companies can reach their consumer base better because their understanding of the consumer market is better. It's a no-brainer.

Women in engineering

Attracting women into STEM fields has proved to be difficult. In European countries, the engineering force has remained on average under 10%. Engineering can be a hard place for women to grow.

More women leave engineering jobs than men do. Research indicates some of the top reasons are: rigid working conditions, lack of advancement and interesting assignments, or low salary. Studies show than one in five women leave because of a lack of a good workplace climate, their boss, or the corporate culture. When it comes to combining motherhood and career in these fields the situation still has a lot of room for improvement. For a female working mother in tech and engineering, a break of two to three years for motherhood may mean a real setback in their career.

Currently many programmes encourage women to pursue engineering studies and retain women engineers in the profession. Governments, UN, UNESCO and numerous private efforts from large companies and universities will help to fulfil this human capital and resource we need.

Women in math

Among STEM fields, one of the lowest percentages of women we find is in mathematics. Out of the total of tenure-track positions, only 15% on average are held by women.

Mathematics has an important impact on the creation of the 4th Industrial Revolution design and applications. It affects our life at a level we are not even aware of. As I moved on in my research, I figured out some of the challenges and searched for possible solutions to this puzzle.

Getting published in the first place is at times a challenging milestone for women to achieve. On average, women participated in only 33% of the published papers in the top-tier journals in the field. Citations are also a big deal and women's papers are less likely to be cited than those of their male counterparts. Citations mean recognition and influence. The numbers are not promising here either.

The number of publications is one of the main metrics of academic success. The academic journals' editorial boards play a key role. Editors hold power over who gets published. If anyone is invited to be part of such a board it's a big deal, it's equivalent to golden circle tickets to your favourite band's once in a lifetime concert! For a mathematician and researcher, that can mean unique professional networking opportunities and a milestone for tenure and promotion. It's an honour. However, less than 10% of all math journal positions are held by women and on average 16% in many natural and life sciences, especially at the editorial leadership (ie associate editors and editors-in-chief).

Generations are shifting gears

Think of this: our workplace today is the most age diverse in history. At least four generations form teams under the same roof today. Due to later retirement, we expect to see even more of that in the future.

Who's who in your team? Perhaps some of your team members are Generation X, like myself (people born between 1965-1980). Or are they part of the two emerging generations: Millennials

(1981-1997) and Generation Z (born after 1998)? Each has specific characteristics that will impact the 4IR.

I have two Generation Z members under my own roof at home, and I am particularly excited to see what kind of impact they will generate when they go and use their power and skills in this new world.

By 2020, all the Millennials will be adults. They will outnumber the Baby Boomer generation. By 2025 they will make up 75% of the workforce. They are digital natives and are overwhelmingly liberal with a low rate of religious belief. If you are a Millennial reading this, you may identify the word impact as a meaningful concept.

I work with hundreds of Millennials, and I see them as a more tolerant and engaged generation. They want to do good things and be well. They have impulse and drive, and when it comes to making business decisions, I see a combination of market value and consciousness. They seek meaning and impact, not simply a quick win. That is perhaps why companies have a hard time retaining them; not because of lack of resilience, but lack of clarity in the company's mission and the impact they create.

Millennials will drive a lot of this transformation while seeking a more holistic approach to life. They are moving away from old models of work-life balance. They search for meaning, purpose and *work-life integration*. They are redefining what success means to them. Other generations operate from a different value perspective when it comes to work recognition and rewards.

1.

WHAT GOT US HERE, WON'T GET US THERE

"We need all hands on deck, and that means clearing hurdles for women and girls as they navigate careers in science, technology, engineering, and math."

MICHELLE OBAMA, AMERICAN LAWYER AND WRITER
WHO SERVED AS FIRST LADY OF THE UNITED STATES

As we enter the 4th Industrial Revolution or 4IR, organisations will face challenges in bringing on board talented people who effectively communicate and work alongside each other. The new digital and technological revolution will increase some of those differences in the future as we transition. One thing is true for all generations: what got us here won't get us where we need and want to go next.

Professionals today need to expand their skill sets to advance in a fast-paced economy.

We will need to develop new maps for the skills that are needed today and will be demanded tomorrow. Machine learning can speed this process. Shifting the skill mix and leveraging it for the future is key. It's time to reinvent alternative education models, professional on-the-job training.

2020 – New set of essential skills

Essential skills from 2020 on	Important skills in 2015
1. Complex problem solving	1. Complex problem solving
2. Critical thinking	2. Coordinating with others
3. Creativity	3. People management
4. People management	4. Critical thinking
5. Coordinating with others	5. Negotiation
6. Emotional intelligence	6. Quality control
7. Judgment and decision-making	7. Service orientation
8. Service orientation	8. Judgment and decision-making
9. Negotiation	9. Active listening
10. Cognitive flexibility	10. Creativity

The world economic forum surveyed 350 executives across nine industries in 15 of the world's biggest economies. They came up with this list as core skills that their organisations will look for in people and talent.

In a world increasingly functioning via artificial intelligence, augmented and virtual reality and robotics, this list reveals what the market will be looking for in humans in the years to come. Surprisingly, at least a third of these skills are not yet listed by employers as key skills today, though they will. Let's invest in becoming future ready. Change won't wait for us.

What is in it for you?

- Exciting opportunities and unique challenges. Transformation at many levels. The 4IR will test both you and me on what we are made of. You can change a fix-mindset, toxic assumptions, systems that no longer serve humankind. You can decide to allow yourself and your ideas to shine and improve, create and generate solutions. In this new hyper-connected world, you can decide to get ready to take risks and try, not in a fearless way, but in spite of fear. You can decide on the impact **you** want to have, and this book helps you remove and overcome challenges that may hinder you in achieving your goals.

- You can decide to sit in the driving seat of the transformational process and head towards construction and creation of a truly sustainable future. Enjoy the perks and merit that go with it and be recognised for it. Not only as team members, but also as decision-makers, creators, inventors and authors of this new reality.

- Finally, you can decide to have an active role defining this new set of values and ethics in a world of ultra-smart intelligent devices, artificial intelligence, and for future generations. Decide how to go forward. Make things happen and don't wait for things to happen in the new 4IR. In the next chapters, I will provide ideas and strategies for you to get what you want.

Be strategic

I want to help you crack the 'code' in this new game. We will go from raising self-awareness to learning new actionable strategies. A new chance to take action and spark ideas to get to your next level. Think of the next chapters as your new Swiss Army knife 4.0 to navigate in STEM fields.

Maya, a client in biotech, said: "This is the first time I feel proud of myself and my puzzle!" Her words at the end of her last coaching session two years ago. Maya had finally got what she wanted. Moreover, she got the staff and lab space she needed for the groundbreaking research she and her team were doing.

Why did she call it her 'puzzle'? It all started when she arrived at my office five months earlier. We met at a Women in Biotech event; she looked drained and, frankly, fatigued. As a mother of two kids in elementary school, she told me that the juggling she was doing was intense. I could relate to that part. She lacked focus and was missing a connection to her loved ones. Interestingly this had nothing to do with her being a mum, or her kids, or the early mornings in the office, or even the tight deadlines. The real reason was that she had recently been passed over for a big promotion, which she had been expecting for a long time. And the worst part is that the guy who got it is someone she helped on-board and trained. What was wrong? She was demotivated, depleted. She was stuck and unhappy.

We had a good talk, and I offered to help. I helped find her missing piece. A strategy. We defined what she wanted, without 'shoulds' and 'coulds'. Rather, what she most wanted from her career. We walked a path identifying what kind of skills were her 'muscle' to overcome challenges. We drew a path, clear enough for her to see the summit, and flexible enough for her to decide where to take a detour along the way to the top. Maya sorted out her puzzle.

I could so relate to her. When I was in IT, at times I saw my career as a messy group of pieces of an organised puzzle. Often parts didn't seem to fit at all and they didn't resemble the picture I thought my career would resemble. Have you ever felt symptoms such as these? Feeling depleted, overtired, distracted, demotivated, unfocused, undervalued. Perhaps you push the snooze button more often, and it's hard to get out of bed and go to work. I know for me, years ago, the anxiety of feeling stuck in a job with no future or vision made me almost nauseous every Sunday evening. My stomach knotted and a sense of agitation got to me, wishing the hours would pass more slowly. After all, I had chosen computer technology for myself.

I now know my indecisiveness came from a lack of clarity. I felt like a failure. I wished I had known this stuff before, when it could have helped. Eventually I looked for mentors, sponsors and support when I needed to. I was fortunate to meet good leaders along the way, observe and learn from them. I made many mistakes that later became lessons. You know what they say, the only real mistake is the one from which we learn nothing.

Numbers speak for themselves, the majority of areas within the STEM fields are male-dominated environments. I coach hundreds of women yearly and the majority of them in tech and engineering. Although you will read several stories of my coachees facing challenges and overcoming them in hostile environments, it's clear not all STEM companies foster an unwelcoming environment. Still, we see worryingly few women in these fields.

The solution lies in a combination of three elements:

- What leadership in organisations can do to attract more women and retain female talent in STEM fields, including new sets of updated policies and rule book.

- Strategies 4.0 that women can use to voice their ideas and get what they need and want. These include self-confidence and courage, and crushing self-doubt.

- The last element is about defeating implicit/unconscious bias in organisations to build working environments where all genders have a chance to flourish. Biases are limiting stereotypes and beliefs that minimise people's potential to make optimal decisions.

Solution 4.0 – A Triangle to thrive in the 4th Industrial Revolution

Key points Chapter 1

- From 2020 on, the top three skills needed will be complex problem solving, critical thinking and creativity.

- What got you where you are today won't get you there, where you want and need to go in the future. You can do it, though you'll need a new set of tools and strategies to get there.

- In order to crack the 'code' in this new game, you'll need a combination of self-awareness, the ability to take risks, courage, upgraded communication skills and a strategic mind. It will be your new Swiss Army knife 4.0.

- Overcoming the challenges of the future lies in everyone's hands. Amassing all the brain power we can get means including the other 50% of the population in all STEM fields: women.

- The solution is a combination of the three elements: inclusive leadership/updated policies in leading organisations, defeating unconscious bias in organisations and finally a set of strategies 4.0 for women to gain confidence and crush self-doubt.

- This book will reveal how to get there.

2.
NO CHANGE
NO GAIN

"Things are always changing. Part of being successful here is being comfortable with not knowing what's going to happen."

SUSAN WOJCICKI, AMERICAN TECHNOLOGY EXECUTIVE,
CEO YOUTUBE

This chapter is going to propel you forward with an invitation to review where you are, what you want, and it will help you raise awareness of where you are dropping the ball and what kind of core strengths already exist in your toolbox. You will learn to harness the power of verbal and non-verbal communication. Do you want to get your papers published? Do you want that promotion and recognition for your work? Great, let's start. You'll get strategies to do exactly that.

It's time we women claim what we want, we have the responsibility to ask for it and the right to get it. It's one of the cornerstones of my role as a business owner. And I know we need to build our confidence to get there and to go as far as we want to go. Even though policies are changing, we can't wait for that to happen for us to achieve our boldest goals. As an entrepreneur myself, I coach leaders in organisations to realise the benefits of flexible models and more welcoming environments, so they succeed in bringing in more women and retaining their talent and value.

This is also a chance to update your career goals. What you once set your mind on may have changed, and it's taking time for you to realise you no longer want or need the same thing. At this point, some of my clients know they want to shift gear, change course and leave what they are doing. That clarity is also valid. A self-assessment of where you are is a good starting point before you decide where and if you want to reach a summit. Let's make sure you are climbing the mountain you want to climb.

A strategy in today's world doesn't look like a bright Google map with a red line and the shortest, most efficient route. A strategy today is a crucial piece of our life and work. On one hand it will be a compass and on the other it will be a flexible element to take advantage of opportunities and avoid traps – nonetheless it's still a traditional roadmap. It's a concept that's agile and adaptable and also aligned. It's not only aligned with what the market needs or wants, it's also aligned to your boldest goals.

I'll be asking you a few critical questions, so you may want to grab a piece of paper and a pen. Make yourself a tea or coffee. I personally find a hot Mexican dark coffee to be a good companion when I am in a self-reflective mood. OK, sometimes it's an icy Margarita if inspiration doesn't flow smoothly. Make yourself comfortable. Follow me in this visualisation exercise. The questions and answers will be related to your present and future professional career. Keep this scope in mind.

Your path doesn't have GPS coordinates – decide where you'll go through self-awareness

Since I am sitting in Switzerland today, it occurred to me that taking an imaginary hike is a good way for you to do this. Get your hiking boots on. Take a backpack with you, make sure it has enough space because you will need to put some new life skills inside.

Summer breeze, sunny day. You can see an open path in front of you. Fresh air and your favourite aromas of nature surround you. Uhm… nice! Keep walking. We are going to make three stops.

The first is a wooden sign on the right side of the road. It reads 'YOUR STRENGTHS'.

Grab that pen. Write as many words under that category that come to mind.

It's important to list things you may be good at, even though you don't necessarily love them. Sometimes you may take strengths for granted because you don't use them all the time or you aren't passionate about them. In this category 'being good at something' might be several things. Don't be modest.

Did you stop listing words? Come on, let me help you. Think of your latest achievements. What strengths and skills did you use to get them?

Think of any recent challenges you overcame. What was the core skill you used to do it?

What about the natural skills you have? Delve deeper, you may even find underlying strengths. Play with me and answer this: what do colleagues, bosses and peers/friends continually praise in you?

When you are doing something and lose track of time, what are you doing? How are you doing it? Finally, mention things that re-energise you when you work on them. Those activities that fill your cup of energy and give good vibes when you do them in the office, your lab or your working area.

Awesome. Take a sip of your drink, keep walking.

You keep walking and you are feeling good. Remembering accomplishments and moments where you've kicked ass before can be an empowering strategy to drive you on.

There's a hiking trail ahead of you. One sign reads 'YOUR NEEDS'.

Let me clarify. Need: something you have to have. Want: something you would like to have.

We won't refer to the human basic needs (shelter, nutrition, basic health, etc.). In this self-reflection exercise, you are looking to move up and beyond of the traditional Maslow's Pyramid of human needs. Life is meant to be lived, not survived.

You are now looking for what you need to thrive and make progress towards your vision. These words are nouns and for now we'll focus on non-tangible needs. Things that matter and money can't buy. Make a list of all the things that must be present for you to feel fulfilled. Here are some ideas: autonomy, fun, space for your work, a sense of respect for your work. Perhaps a clean environment, clear rules of the game, power, wealth, recognition, and projects that are challenging, sleep, smiley colleagues, a mentor. Be courageous and name what you really *need*. Great! Keep walking.

Next stop on your trail. This time your sign is in a clear meadow. It reads 'YOUR WANTS'.

Sometimes it isn't so easy to know what you *really* want. Often it's easier to know what you don't want. Think of it. What do you really, *really* want? Can you describe that in a few words? I mean the really big stuff you want to get. I'm not talking about what others expect you to do and have. Nor am I talking about 'shoulds' or 'musts' that you or others may expect from yourself. Not the things you are settling for now to dodge having to ask for or avoid getting into trouble over. What do you *really* want?

What's on your mind? Let's get more concrete and real. This is not the time to be modest in your vision or to get constrained when building your vision. Here's where I'll ask you to recalibrate. What you used to want, is it still current? Is this the time to update your goals? Do you still want the same thing? If you are not sure, ask 'why' you want something. The answer to that question may be revealing at this point. When you decide you want something, think big. Some of these 'wants' are things you'll be perfectly comfortable saying 'I want this…'. Some things though, on this list, should almost be making you nervous. Those are the kind of things that you know you'll have to stretch yourself, to go the extra mile, to get creative on the way, and it won't necessarily be easy, though it will be worth it!

You're doing great. We're almost there. The new sign on your hiking path reads 'YOU in 24 MONTHS'.

You are about to get more clarity and more strategic about your professional wants and needs. Where and how do you see yourself in 24 months from today? In the past, a strategy had a more long-term timescale. Part of your upgraded version of tools is to strategise for a timescale you will work towards in this immediate period. These goals are also related to your impact. Use the words that describe the role you will hold. The place where you'll be, location, financial achievements, and even the personal situation that will best serve your goals. Imagine, also, who is working with you and what you will be working on. In this image, how do you look? What sort of words describe your state of mind and mood? What type of skills will you master in that time? And what other kind of things you know you will have got by then? Make a mental picture of that image.

Your new compass

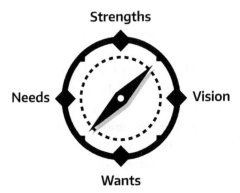

Look at your list. It now has four sections. Strengths, wants, needs and your vision for the future. It's your new *compass*. A life compass which can make your decision-making process easier from now on. Many of us, including me, lose track of our wants and needs when we get distracted, unfocused or in autopilot mode. As a result we make decisions that are not aligned with what we really wish for ourselves in the future.

Whenever you are offered a new project, job, proposal, and even life changes, you can look at your compass. Is it aligned? Would that step take you closer to achieving your vision and boldest goals? Every relevant decision you make does that. It gets you closer to or further from your most ambitious goals.

Personally, I need to check my 'compass' and remind myself about this before committing to new big projects. For example, as I write this book for you, I've been requested (at least three times) to work with digital companies in Asia, which I would love to accept and add value. Hard to say no to these requests now, though it's crucial I carry on this project. The trick to achieve this is pinned to my wall. I've got a handwritten note my kids wrote reminding me to go on, and my favourite quote by Maya Angelou staring at me: "If you don't like something, change it. If you can't change it, change your attitude." It's a little piece that keeps me on track, so I chose wisely.

What would keep you on track? What sort of structure (image, stimulus, quote, song, picture, icon, item, a picture of your sheet with the four sections on, etc.) can remind you of this vision of yours? Choose one. It doesn't have to be elegant or perfect. It's simple. Put it somewhere where it makes your decision-making process easier, or have it with you. Whenever I coach women, at the end I give them a small reminder (a bracelet) with a simple engraved message – the word is Courage. Courage is not being fearless, it's attempting to do something in spite of the fact you may be afraid because it's important, or the right thing to do.

Sometimes less is more. Your goals and dreams are not always about having *more*. In fact, sometimes they are about having less, slowing down, or doing less. Example? One of my goals for the last two years has not been to work more on challenging projects, it was to regain sleep in my life, to have clarity and be healthy. Therefore, your career goals may have milestones such as taking on fewer irrelevant projects and aim at getting more challenging, interesting projects. It's maybe about saying *'no'* to unreasonable requests, setting boundaries and regaining your personal and professional power.

Now, let's upgrade your toolbox to get what you want with less trouble. I want you to get more buy-in from your stakeholders. I want you to reduce resistance and conflict in your life. You can move forward, up or jump and move to the sides/change gear if that's what you want. Interested? Keep going.

Key points Chapter 2

- No change no gain. Before you can decide to strategise and get to the next level, you can take a good look at where you are in your career, what you *really* want, and a clear goal to achieve within 12-24 months. Strategy is how you will get there.

- The new compass you created in this chapter is a personal map. It will ease your future decision-making. It's a visual reminder of your strengths, vision, needs and wants.

- Establish the connection to yourself. Be brutally honest with yourself about what really matters to you, and know yourself. Achieving this can be life-career changing.

3.
DO'S - YOUR NEW SWISS ARMY KNIFE 4.0

"We must have perseverance and above all confidence in ourselves."

MARIE SKŁODOWSKA CURIE, FRENCH-POLISH PHYSICIST AND CHEMIST,
NOBEL PRIZE WINNER IN TWO DIFFERENT SCIENCES

Actionable strategies and new tools

This chapter will give you a set of easy how-to tools. You'll be able to use this in your very next meeting, conference call or email. Trust me, these tools will make your life easier.

Imagine you are about to have a meeting with your main stakeholder about a new proposal or idea. Or perhaps you are about to make an important decision and communicate it to your team. This is a key moment to include the three Cs of communication: be concise, concrete and clear.

Concise: say it using the fewest possible words while still being effective. It's timesaving and it highlights the main message.

Concrete: cover particular points and paint a clear picture, not fuzzy or general. You'll be perceived as confident. Use facts and figures and avoid being misinterpreted.

Clear: focus on one specific message or goal at a time. It's easy to follow. Complete your ideas using a clear outline. Use correctness and accuracy.

Now, let's dive in and review the "Hows"

Keep the big picture in mind and let's be action-oriented. It's easy to get tangled up in details, especially if you are presenting your big idea. Part of coming across as a strategic, valuable contributor is being able to get the 'helicopter view'. Explain it as simply as possible. Use analogies and effective language. Be direct, and articulate complex ideas in a simple way.

Pick a high visibility goal and get focused on achieving it. Make sure this links to the organisation's main objectives. You need to be able to articulate how your goal links to the big picture.

Use this magic word. I discovered this in a short article on leadership research a few years back. Studies show this word will reap you tremendous dividends if you use it in a smart way at key moments. The word is *strategic* – in fact, all variations of the word root: strategy, strategical, strategically. You and I know it as a business term, right? It turns out the word is accredited to the Greek as *strategos* which means 'general' and later the Romans used *strategia* to refer to territories under their control. It turns out that using this keyword at moments when the stakes are high pays off. Those moments can be: important meetings, appraisals, relevant email, negotiations, etc. It increases the perception on how others appreciate you as a strategic contributor. Voilà! In addition, all you are doing is expressing your ideas whilst raising perception of confidence and clarity.

Hold the floor with muscular language

Once you've got their attention, use proactive and active language. Express your ideas using authoritative statements, avoid language that makes you sound as if you are 'walking on eggshells'. Instead of simply agreeing with others, build on their ideas.

Examples:

Instead of	*Say*
I agree	I agree completely, and this is why…
Perhaps we can...?	Here is an idea or here is a plan
What if we maybe...?	I recommend or I suggest…
Yes, but…	Yes, and…
How about...?	I strongly suggest or recommend…

Strive for excellence in all you do. Notice I didn't say work towards perfectionism. Two different things.

Increase your financial acumen. My what? You may think that as you are a scientist, a researcher or specialist, you should know these things? I say yes. It's part of the business quality skills you don't want to ignore. It's having a sense of the effective use of resources, standards and metrics that matter in your business or industry. It refers to being able to manage resources – especially financial resources and budgeting – and also the way you get to understand management trends in your field.

Try these things for the next few months. You'll raise a perception of having a solid presence.

Join the dots

Join your ideas and initiatives to business goals or clear KPIs that your organisation values. Here is a clear example that Laura, head of HR at an engineering company, successfully used to get buy-in from the executive board team. Instead of promoting an initiative for 'more inclusive culture' (which had been shut down years before), she presented it as a strategic initiative. She said: *"Listen team, due to our current talent shortage, I recommend to look at a human capital plan for next year. When we achieve an inclusive, learning-based culture, aligned with our growth strategy, we will get this done. And here's how it can look like…"* Voilà. That sounded proactive and openly joined strategic business goals to her initiative.

Responding v reacting

When was the last time you snapped at someone because you were tired, hungry or stressed? I bet you can remember at least once when that happened. We all have triggers that detonate reactions.

The trouble is when anger or fear take over your steering wheel. Are you driving or is it your anger or insecurity doing it?

I'll give you a few tips that can help. I was brought into one of the largest pharmaceutical companies in the world because, apparently, one of their most senior female leaders had 'issues' (according to her HR department). I met Emma and I was expecting a difficult, even aggressive, personality. She entered the room, sat on the chair and actually looked rather timid and quiet, in my view. It turns out she had been putting up with unreasonable requests and tasks that were not part of her job description for over two years. If that wasn't bad enough, the day came when, in a steering committee meeting that had run over lunchtime, she was interrupted several times. She lost it. She raised her voice, she snapped at others and went on to complain not only about the topic in hand. She complained about every single time she had held her tongue and withheld comments and ideas because of the fear of being attacked or ignored. She accused her colleagues of ignoring her contributions and, of course, of interrupting her. Silence in the room. She lost it, and when she felt tears welling up, she left the room. And now we were face to face in order to handle this so-called 'difficult' personality.

Here's the thing, when we are under attack or undervalued and frustrated, our reptilian brain goes to work. There are two primary reactions to this: fight or flight (escape). The first one breaks relationships, ruins reputations, and ultimately doesn't fix problems. The second leaves you frustrated and unvalued, unheard and, over time, drains your energy. Until one day, just like Emma, your reptilian brain takes the wheel and drives off. Bad results.

Emma learned that there is a definite difference between reactions and responses. The word response comes from responsibility, the ability to respond. She offered a sincere apology to people that this incident affected. Even if she thought her complaints were justified, the situation got heated, therefore this step was important.

Once we identified exactly *what* sent her spinning, it was time to implement some tactics to ensure she wouldn't have that same reaction again.

You don't need to know all the nitty-gritty about the brain, though these nuggets can help you next time you feel like you are about to lose it.

When you feel threatened, frightened or at risk, your first two primary reactions will kick in: fight or flight. In the past, these reactions have helped human beings to preserve life. In the wild animal kingdom, this warning system and our quick reactions are part of the reason why we are here. However, during a status meeting, a presentation or a telephone call, our life *per se* is not at stake, is it? Allowing your reptilian brain to decide in those situations is not useful and it sabotages your results. It's your job to make sure you get to respond. How do you get to do that?

Here are a few steps that will help

Take a good look at you and your triggers

Triggers are things/events that cause us to test our balance and temper. The first four categories to start reviewing yours: hunger, anger, loneliness and tiredness (or *HALT* an easy acronym to remember those initials). I use this tool to coach leaders and entire teams. Everyone has an 'Aha' moment when they recognise theirs. What are your top one or two triggers so far? Take note.

Other triggers are things people do. Your job is to identify those accurately. Here are some examples: you get triggered when you are interrupted, threatened or attacked, or feel you are being mistreated or criticised about your work, to be called a specific way/name, pushed aside, screamed at, ignored. Or past experiences that come alive when you experience something similar in the present. You get the point. Identify what bugs you the most. Once you list those things, it's going to be easier for you to get behind the wheel, because what happens next determines the future of your relationships and your outcomes.

Now you are in a more advantageous position to take control and mitigate your triggers. Example: my triggers have to do with hunger and time. That means I need to make sure my need for healthy food is covered. I don't skip meals or prioritise any meeting or session if I haven't eaten. You really wouldn't want to work with me hungry. So, I plan ahead.

What can you do to mitigate and reduce the risk of your reptilian brain getting behind the wheel when those triggers occur? Once you know your triggers, here are some next steps you can take.

In and out

Breathe in slowly for three seconds, hold it for three seconds and then release it in three seconds. I coach women do this in my training, I call it 3 x 3 x 3. Do it before you hit the send button, before you enter that room and talk to your boss or that incompetent jerk who upsets you during those status meetings, or that one PhD know-it-all who criticises your work systematically. It works. It helps the executive centre of your brain get enough oxygen to think. It gives you the power to shift from reacting to responding. It works wonders. It's when you invite the lizard brain to sit in the back seat of the car; you are driving.

Take a break and get fresh air

Imagine someone says something inappropriate/displays lousy behaviour or is utterly stupid and you know it's one of your triggers. Allow yourself to gain some distance and time, literally step away and take a few seconds or even minutes. If the situation allows you to leave the room, take a time-out, find a safe place and regain focus. Ideally get some fresh air before continuing a meeting, a discussion or negotiation. You'll be surprised how perspectives can shift when you change the scenario, even for a few moments. It's my experience that many of my female clients don't feel entitled to take a little time out before responding to requests or making a decision, or even answering a question. Most times you do have that possibility. If you need to, do it. Take it.

Control your day, or it will control you

If your trigger is lack of sleep, it messes you up. Don't schedule meetings at certain times when you know you'll have to sacrifice sleep time, or on weekends. If your trigger is loneliness, which is reportedly one of the most dangerous reasons to feel disempowered, and get sick, then don't wait until it's too late and you feel depleted. Look for support, ask for help, see people who re-energise you and avoid those who don't.

Shake it

Exercises and meditation are some of the most effective ways to get hold of your reactions and turn them into responses. I don't care if it's Zumba or boxing, taking walks in the woods, taking the stairs, or sweating your pants off in a kick-box class, but move it girl! The benefits of doing sport and moving come in handy when controlling your triggers in the long run. Your feel-good neurotransmitters, called endorphins, get pumped. As you practise this more regularly, you'll see a long-lasting level of energy that results in more optimism and you can remain calm, clear and collected under pressure.

In the next section, you'll get techniques that will help you to have a strong presence under pressure and to express your ideas with clarity.

The aim of communication is not to be heard, it's that others actually understand you

I recently had the chance to coach the head of a research and development department in a multinational in Zurich. Beatrice is smart, insightful and has a lovely personality. One of her many assets is the art of humour. When something throws her off balance, she tries to look for a quick solution. She tries to see the positive in almost every situation, even though she was struggling with the perception that several of her male engineers had of her. For some reason, they showed a lack of trust in her knowledge when she spoke, especially about technical details, as if she wasn't someone they could rely on. She wasn't aware of what she was doing in those moments, so she brought me in and introduced me as her consultant. I was able to see her in action. It's called shadow-coaching.

I followed her for an entire day. I noticed how warm and empathetic she was towards her team. She listened to other people and made insightful, valuable remarks, though I noticed that whenever her engineers were speaking, they would avoid her and instead look at her report, Dirk, the second in command. They seemed to feel more comfortable and trusted him more. In fact, it almost looked like he was the person in charge. I noticed this even made him a bit uncomfortable; the uninvited attention stressed him out. Interestingly he didn't have the answers, because those came from Beatrice. What was going on?

I then started to uncover the reasons. I observed how Beatrice was coming across. Voilà, I got it. I spotted a couple of things that, although small, were making her look and sound insecure. It wasn't the content, it was the way it was delivered.

Remember, I don't 'fix' women. As a coach, I hold up a mirror that allows women to observe themselves and calibrate the impact that each of their behaviours has on their outcomes. Simple. Beatrice wanted to be taken into account, to be seen as the leader of her team and as a reliable contributor. I couldn't work on the other guys or her team. My contribution was to Beatrice. So, let's see what we did.

Beatrice communicated her ideas in the following order. First, using additional disclaimers, while keeping her hands where I couldn't see them, under the table, or at times she'd fidget with a beautiful piece of jewellery that competed with her message. Second, I noticed that when she was asked questions, she was breaking eye contact with the enquirer. I twice caught an interaction where she was apparently under pressure. Feeling stressed resulted in her having a nervous smile, fast speech and scrambled ideas.

Tame your nerves in three steps

I coached Beatrice to remember three simple steps. Now I'd like you to learn these simple steps to address any question especially when **you** are under pressure:

1. Pause: Pause for three to five seconds before saying anything.

   Beatrice: 1-2-3-4… "Paul…"

   Awkward? Only in Beatrice's mind. To her it seemed like a long time, especially under pressure. Our perception of time is distorted when we are under pressure. It actually sounds like a natural pause to the interviewer.

   This simple technique helps project more confidence and control over the situation. It gets the responder extra time to think and deliver ideas in a coherent way.

2. Paraphrase: Repeating back the question concisely captures the essence of their enquiry and it helps you gain clarity and time. To paraphrase well, add no emotional energy, sarcasm

or irony to your speech. Example: *"Paul, you are referring to the results of the second quarter, correct?"*

3. Three chunks only: Working memory refers to the temporary storage of information, how much information we can pay attention to and manipulate. Recent observations show that people's working memory helps them remember up to three or even four items at a time. This matters because even if your answer covers many points, group them all into three main categories. Present your ideas orderly, one by one, while you effectively gesture a timeline or order. Make sure your first answer doesn't exceed 60-90 seconds. If it's longer than that, stop and check for understanding. Create a dialogue-like conversation. Most times, it isn't a one-sided interrogatory.

Who's got 'gravitas'?

Think of someone you admire in your field because of the way she/he carries her/himself. That person's someone who's a unique combo: knowledgeable and yet approachable. She enters the room and heads turn. People gravitate towards that person in a conversation circle. That person has a *wow* factor. Some people call this 'executive presence', I prefer the word 'gravitas' (from Latin: weight and serious). We use it to notice someone with a solid presence, whose opinions have credibility and substance or depth of personality.

Gravitas is often associated with perceptions of influence and authority. It does this even despite their levels of experience, formal hierarchy, education or skills. Your level of presence or gravitas can override other attributes. Some people seem to be born with natural gravitas. Fortunately, it is also something that can be developed.

Let's get back to the person you are thinking of. Her or his presence is substantial and yet friendly enough that you want to talk to her/ him. A person whose attitude and energy makes you acknowledge her/his presence in a room. You can't but look at her/him or listen to her/him when she/he speaks. Got someone like that in your mind? It could be in your present or past jobs, or perhaps your school time or in your professional circle. In my courses, many women name their mothers, grandmothers or teachers as people whom they admire and have this type of powerful presence. Get someone in mind, it's essential.

Imagine that person entering the room. How does she/he walk? How does she/he look? What is she/he wearing or doing as she/he crosses the room? What leads you to choose her/him as a reliable, competent and approachable person?

A person's gravitas draws people to want to talk to them or work with them. Let's deconstruct this and figure this one. Why? Because I know how relevant it is when it comes to you getting what you want. Let's see, your gravitas/executive presence is a combination of these factors:

- Confidence and ability to cope with pressure.

- Your ability to show decisiveness and integrity.

- And your capacity to show emotional intelligence and express clear ideas.

That is all embedded in an effective set of communication skills and suitable appearance.

What happens when these factors come together with consistency over time? Your personal brand shines. You may be thinking: *Do you mean, Gabriela, I have a personal brand?* Yes, we all have one, and the question is: what is it saying about you? Your personal brand is a promise of value. What people see in you that tells them what they can expect when they work with you.

When your body language speaks louder than your words

"Your actions speak so loudly, I cannot hear what you are saying."
Ralph Waldo Emerson (philosopher and poet) used to say.

In Berlin, 2017, I was the keynote speaker at one of the largest virtual reality conferences to date. The aim: to inspire engineers to create products and solutions that also include empathy in all new technologies and augmented reality. Audience members: all engineering fields with analytical minds and many sceptical about the power of non-verbal communication. I am introduced, I take the stage at an energetic pace, open posture, big smile, shoulders back, and in a provoking move, I place my hands on my hips, feet slightly apart, chin slightly up, no smile, and with a loud, strong tone, I said: "I'm shy!" Laughter rang out around the room for a few moments. Then silence. I took a few steps and then stopped. I hunched back, slumped shoulders, fidgeted nervously, made nervous, repetitive moves with my hands. Finally, using a low volume, I said: "I'm confident." Laughter again. My audience was letting me know they weren't buying any of those sentences. Mission accomplished. I made my point right at the beginning.

I asked: "What! You don't believe me! Why?" Someone shouted out from the first row: "You don't look like that." "Exactly!" I said. "Your brain is looking for congruency between my body language and my words." I went on to demonstrate why this is important.

During my years as a technology specialist, I used to think that words and content were absolute power! I thought body language and voice projection were 'nice to have'. Over time, I realised they are by far the most powerful elements in communication. If you are like me, you also need evidence about this.

Many body language studies made by recognised institutions have debated the exact impact of body language and voice over words.

People, including Amy Cuddy (American social psychologist, famous TED speaker), at Princeton University and other recognised social scientists at the University of Jerusalem and Harvard, have worked on this. They carried out experiments to prove and raise awareness of the power of body language in conveying messages that are believable and perceived as valid.

I am sure you want to be seen as a trustworthy scientist, IT specialist or manager. Then you want to make body language your superpower.

We now know that body language and voice qualities count for over 90% of the effectiveness of communication. When the visuals are missing (over the phone for example) your voice gains importance. When it's only text, of course, your words gain power, and yet we can tell the attitude and energy of the person who sent us a warm or a nasty email, can't we?

Let's use body language strategically, especially at key moments. Example: you are under pressure, someone asks you a challenging question either to bug you or simply turn on the heat. Using powerful, confident body language will help you convey your answer in a way that is reliable and believable.

Another example: you need to give delicate feedback to someone or talk about something where you may expect resistance; your body language and voice quality will largely determine the response/reaction of the person.

Careful, I'm not suggesting that you learn how to lie. These things, like many tools, can work both ways. I am saying watch what your body is telling your stakeholders, what your tone is communicating, even if you think you are using the right words. Think about alignment. Look, say and act the way you want to be perceived. You are powerful and you can make a conscious decision about this. In conclusion, it's not only what you say, but how you say it.

First thing: the blink effect

This effect happens when your brain goes through a mental process, which rapidly and automatically helps you decide something, even though you have relatively little information on hand. Understanding this mental process can help you realise what kind of signals and information you want to send out to the world about who you are and what you stand for. It will impact everything, from first impressions to your elevator pitch.

At the beginning of my career in IT, I tried everything when it came to my outfits. There were times when I wanted to fit in and blend in well. There were times when I thought that was nonsense, then I wanted to stand out. I tried the dark suit, the nice dress, the high heels and the flats. I didn't have a clue as to how to dress to meet clients, to give a presentation or at an office party. I didn't know there was such a thing as smart business casual, or the many variations on that. I used to believe that it was all about my intellect. I thought that dressing up to give a presentation was trying to convince people through my looks and not my knowledge. Well, guess what? I now know it's the whole package that can help anyone get the job done. Professional business attire doesn't define your competence; even so, it goes a long way towards influencing the impression your boss, peers and customers have about your capabilities and professionalism.

I'm not an image consultant. In fact, I often consult other people to get advice about my different outfits. One of my friends who is, in fact, an image consultant, shared her opinion: due to the wide variety of options we women have to dress for in the workplace, she pointed out how picking the right outfit for a special professional moment can be a minefield. Getting one thing wrong can sabotage our appearance and be perceived differently from how we want to come across. Here are some tips I found to be super useful.

The visualisation effect

I found this out when I was helping an HR manager. I supported the hiring process to get good people on board as employees. One of the common arguments after some interviews was: *"I can't imagine that person dealing with my most important Class A client under pressure!"* What he was signalising was what many of us do unconsciously when we select partners, employees, etc. We need to be able to 'see' them in our mind, imagining possible future scenarios, overcoming a challenge or dealing with a situation, to know how solid they are. If we are able to picture them solving those possible challenges, it is going to influence our decision.

Unluckily some of the candidates in the process didn't appear to be as solid for the position in person as they looked on paper. The difference was the way they carried themselves; some had dressed for a typical day at the office instead of for a promotion interview.

How would you like to be perceived in a negotiation or presentation, under pressure? Whatever your answer is, make it easier for others to 'imagine' you handle such situations like a pro – which you are. Like a high performer and valuable contributor with gravitas/ executive presence in that hypothetical future scenario.

Your handshake: the make-it or break-it factor

Handshakes do matter. One thing I've learned while coaching women worldwide is that whether we like it or not, people quickly get an idea of who you are and how a handshake is the beginning of a relationship. It's culturally influenced, and it helps the brain quickly match expectations or past experience. It sets the tone in many ways and sends a message about your personal power and confidence. In western cultures, a good handshake usually doesn't exceed three seconds, it's firm, dry and it goes up and down as a sign of mutual respect. What is your handshake saying about you?

And more interestingly, is it saying what you want to convey to your stakeholders/peers/colleagues/ decision-makers?

I've been training women in STEM fields for years. Here are a few tips for you, mainly because you are most likely working in a male-dominated environment. On a scale of 1 to 10, 10 being the top number, you aim at a solid 7-8 in intensity. Number 10 is a handshake that is overpowering and cracks people's knuckles. Zero is a dead-fish handshake, which leaves people wondering about someone's competence and reliability. Be wise and adapt this step to other cultures and regions in the world. Observe, wait and act accordingly. Your handshake can be the first step you take to let people know you are present; you are confident, approachable, engaged and ready to contribute.

Slow down, Speedy Gonzalez

Let's go back to that person you admire (previous chapter). Again, have a picture of him/her in your mind. Now, think of how they move, walk and gesture. How fast do they do that? Do they speak rapidly, run around and rush into the room as quickly as Speedy Gonzalez (little mouse in cartoons that ran around like crazy). Now, the person you admire, would he/she show an apologetic attitude while quickly taking a seat? Nope. I bet not. People who have this effect of presence and poise move s l o w l y. It's a sign of respect for themselves and also it comes across as being natural, it also increases the perception of competence and gravitas. It's not about walking arrogantly or in slow motion. It's when you take your time to arrive, to move, to raise your hand, to take your seat, to pause, to answer, you are sending a message that says 'I'm collected, cool, confident and I enjoy being here with you'. No rush. No worries. This inspires a perception of self-power and calmness at the same time. Conclusion: practise walking slowly.

When you move restlessly and rapidly, the perception you give is that you are not that important, you are coming across as apologetic for being present and certainly not a powerful player in the room. This is a hard habit to battle. If you are someone who's used to speeding up when walking and talking, you need to know this works against the perception of gravitas and the substantial presence you want to have.

How you sound

Your voice is such a powerful weapon or tool. Every time you express your ideas in meetings, calls and presentations, your tone, word emphasis, speed, pitch and volume often say more than your words.

Emphasis

The tone is like a 'plug-in' in your vocal power. It helps you express sadness, a warm feeling or anger. When you put it together with other qualities like speed, you can convey even more. As a child, I recall my mum and teachers calling my full name in a loud, firm tone. I knew I was in trouble. It was all about the tone. You can use this little trick to increase a sense of presence and gravitas to your benefit. You can project confidence and sound like a trustworthy individual and avoid sounding nervous and inexperienced.

When you use emphasis in your sentences, you can change the meaning of your convictions. This little trick can save you headaches. By using emphasis correctly, you can avoid or decrease conflict and reduce resistance amongst stakeholders. This is an example I coached my client Emma on. Whenever she gave feedback to her team, she'd use sentences like this:

- *I* don't think you analysed our Q1 report (someone else said it)

- I don't *think* you analysed our Q1 report (I guess, but I don't think so)

- I don't think *you* analysed our Q1 report (someone else must have analysed the report)

- I don't think you *analysed* our Q1 report (the person did something else with the Q1 report other than analysing it)

- I don't think you analysed *our* Q1 report (the person analysed someone else's report)

- I don't think you analysed our *Q1* report (the person analysed another of our reports, not Q1)

The emphasis you use really makes a difference. Even when you think that the words you are choosing are correct, if you are still experiencing resistance and low levels of buy-in from your team, take a look at the emphasis you are choosing.

Bond, James Bond, rule

Everyone remembers how the guy introduces himself in those classic films. Did he sound like he was asking anyone about his name? Or did he sound like someone who introduced himself with confidence? The second one, right? Bond must have known about the damage that *uptalk* does to your credibility. Uptalk is when you raise your intonation at the end of a declarative sentence. So it sounds like you are asking instead of stating something, it damages your credibility. Use the Bond, James Bond, rule.

Maya, the powerhouse woman I told you about previously, used to present her ideas like this before our work together: *"I have an idea? I feel that if we, like, take care of phase 2 critical issue first?"* (using an uptalk and doubtful style). Maya wasn't even aware she was sabotaging her credibility. She raised self-awareness of this little bad habit. It took a conscious effort to correct this habit though now she sounds like she means it. She noticed how she was no longer interrupted or challenged when introducing her ideas. Try it. It'll pay off for the rest of your life at work and anywhere else.

Do this short, powerful exercise with me. Grab your smartphone, record your voice during this exercise. Introduce yourself as you normally do. Name, last name and position. Listen to yourself. How confident and friendly do you sound? Do it again and this time slow down. A little pause between Name. Last name. Position. Using the Bond rule is much better when you introduce yourself. It gives people the benefit of understanding your name clearly. You sound important and collected. Now, get that intonation down on the *last syllable* of the last word in each sentence.

You may discover that you introduce yourself with a subtle uptalk at first! Hi, I'm Gabriela Mueller? (uptalk) and after a little bit of practice, Hi! I'm Gabriela (micro-pause) Mueller (the last syllable goes down). It's not a question, it's an affirmative statement.

You know who does this pretty well? A journalist on a serious news broadcast. Why? Her credibility is at stake. Can you imagine anyone on BBC International saying something like this: Good morning? Welcome? We have some breaking news coming in from the Middle East? (using a constant uptalk). Nope. You wouldn't believe a thing.

This skill – especially on the phone – can be the difference between getting people's approval and trust, or not. When you are introducing yourself to anyone it can make the difference between them engaging with you and taking you seriously, or ignoring you. When giving a presentation it can make the difference between hooking your audience's attention in the first few seconds, or losing them as they decide to pull out their smartphones and start texting. Trust me. It's that important.

Getting rid of the uptalk is one of the most challenging bad habits I coach women in the workplace. Perhaps the root of the problem is thinking that the uptalk intonation is going to soften a message, or will make a person sound *nicer*, whereas in fact it decreases the importance of the message and damages credibility. You and your ideas are too important to lose your power when speaking. Remember, Bond, James Bond.

Zzzzzz... Does your voice have the effect of a sleeping pill?

Some people's monotonous speaking pattern may feel like a way to kill an audience's attention and focus. When they speak, spectators go straight to dreamland. The trick? Mix different speeds, tones, volumes and use emphasis wisely. An easy way to do this: in every sentence, you notice there's *one* word that gains importance according to the meaning of the sentence. That's the one word you want to stress with either volume or emphasis. Easy, right? One word per sentence or thought.

Words have power, choose them wisely

Working with leaders around the world, most of whom are women, I've noticed great leaders and professionals understand the power of the spoken word. I'd like to raise self-awareness of the power you are exercising when you speak. Your words influence others. Choose them carefully so you get what you want.

When I moved to Switzerland in the 90s and knowing how much I wanted to express my ideas and thoughts, I studied German with the determination of a wild horse. I nailed four hours at school daily. After almost two years I reached a level where I was comfortable sharing my ideas at work and socially. To my disappointment, this wasn't enough for most social interactions, because in the Swiss-German part of Switzerland, people communicate using a Swiss-German dialect. They learn this 'by ear', it's not written down. That challenge would take me a few years to overcome.

Yes, some frustration along the way. Yet, I did. I understand most Swiss-German dialects and I communicate my ideas to the best of my ability and continue learning. Choosing words wisely is key, whether in your mother tongue or not.

When it comes to words, I'm not only talking about the words you say to the world. I'm also including those you use to talk to yourself. Some of the women I've coached say to me: "I wouldn't allow anyone to talk to me the way I talk to myself." Which words are you using for yourself when you fail or make a mistake? And when you succeed at something?

The myth about the number of words

Ever since I was a young IT specialist, I have heard myths like this: *Women are good communicators and guys not so much, they are better at other things like execution, and decision-making.* Men, in many ways, aren't expected to have great communication skills for some reason. As a coach and trainer, I've looked into serious research carried out in this regard. I've yet to find solid reasons behind that false belief. Both genders speak, full stop. That's a fact. Now, there are interesting findings that prove women get less air-time in meetings than men and that men are also more prolific in forums and conferences.

Now think about this piece of data: even though it has been hard to prove due to cultural and personal variances, the average human has been shown to speak anything between 7,000 and 20,000 words a day. That's a lot of words, right?

Which words move you and your results forward? Which words make you pull back or feel insecure? The type of language you use can help shift your mind and your results. The words you attach to your work and your experience will also determine outcomes. The words you choose also help others shape an idea of who you are, and you will be treated accordingly.

Increase your influence and network wisely – use D E E P approach

By now I'm sure you know that getting what you want is not only about merits and a proven work record. It's going to require more than having the right credentials or qualifications. And we agreed that what you want can come in many forms: money, recognition, resources, flexible hours and challenging projects, more 'me-time', more office space, more visibility. Whatever it is you want, it's going to require advanced skills.

In order for you to get recognised as a go-to person and having that respect as a professional, so that others seek your advice and guidance, you need to have influence. In order to motivate your colleagues and superiors to support your initiative and ideas, you need influence. You need the influence to change minds and have an effect on people.

You can use my **DEEP** tool. It's an acronym that covers the four aspects of influence

DEEP: Delivery – Emotion – Expertise – Power. Easy to remember, right? Harvard Business Review reports list them and I wanted you to remember them easily, so DEEP is the acronym I prefer to use when I coach women in STEM fields.

DEEP Delivery. It's the communication between people, the actions and behaviours people adopt when talking to each other. It's a dance. Now, Latin dance has always been a passion of mine, and even though I'm not talking about 'dancing' with your stakeholders, I am referring to that subtle layer of human interaction. Think of it as a frame of behaviours. Each person has one. The way they talk, move, speak, approach a topic, their energy and attitude. When two people are attempting to influence one another, you can see these two frames dancing together. These are all verbal and non-verbal signs that a person can emit (hand gestures, eye contact, nodding, breathing, body posture, stance, facial expressions, voice, etc.).

When a conversation is going well and develops into one side it is naturally influenced by the other, you notice the way the speakers may mirror each other, imitating energy and even gestures. Should the conversation not go so well, you will notice how the two bodies distance themselves from each other, standing at angles to each other (not directly facing each other), adopting closed postures and breaking eye contact.

This element by itself usually isn't enough to influence others, even though it's a mighty contributing factor. You also need some of the other three elements.

DEEP Emotion. Passion and enthusiasm are hard to beat. Recall a time when someone was so passionate about something that you became interested and wanted to hear more. You may think that too much passion is counterproductive. Yes, if it's not supported by other elements and a good delivery, it can be overwhelming. Though without it, the conviction of your ideas and solutions will be missing. You want to add the right amount of enthusiasm to your ideas when you prepare a delivery. These elements can count (in my eyes, as a coach) for at least half of your success. Emotion needs to be culturally adapted since different regions of the world have different flavours of it. Observe, adapt smartly.

DEEP Expertise. Your know-how. The stuff at which you are an expert. I don't doubt that your expertise is solid and vast. Though expertise without the other elements is not always heard. Can you recall some of your professors in school who only wanted to offer knowledge? No energy, no enthusiasm, no empathy, though they were the gurus on their subjects. You probably learned from them, though in a competitive, rapidly changing world, this element by itself is no longer enough. Nowadays, organisations, your stakeholders and even you, will all want more than expertise alone. So, we need more tools.

DEEP Power. Yes, positional power is an element of influence. If you have it, influencing others may become an easier task. In fact, people in a position of power tend to speak longer, interrupt more often and usually drive the conversation. Power also draws attention, so it eases the path to exercise influence. Also consider your own personal power, regardless of the hierarchical power you may hold in your organisation.

A recent example of this was given to me by a relatively young woman who welcomed me at the reception of one of the largest food companies in the world. The fact that she wasn't at the top of the organisation chart didn't seem to play any role in the way she carried herself. She was using every bit of her personal power to signalise her job was important. She had executive presence, talked and presented herself in a confident manner. On the contrary, one of the C-suite members at the same company came across as someone whose elevated hierarchical position was perhaps the only reason why people showed him support. He was lacking communication skills, emotion and passion. Good news is that you know this, you can use both personal and formal power to gain influence.

Influence v authority

Regardless of where you are in the organisation, know this: you may have the authority and lack influence, or vice versa. Authority may command obedience though it's often not sustainable. When authority and power want to exert influence without the other elements, they drive talent away and limit creativity and innovation in teams. On the other hand, when influence has a healthy mix of these four elements, it takes on its own flavour and people respond better.

Influence v manipulation

If you are thinking this could be manipulative, I want to ease your mind, it's not. Manipulation by exerting devious attitudes or practices over a person for your own advantage is a misleading way to deal with people. It is risky, not sustainable and it kills trust. When you influence others, you get them to want to react, think, do, or believe in the way you want them to. It's a shift of opinion or mindset on others while revealing the useful information that serves both to make a decision. A life skill that goes beyond your career.

We always influence with our words and acts. If you are a parent, like me, you will see your actions speak louder than words and influence your kids' behaviour in a more direct way than anything else. As a professional, you'll be influencing others by modelling behaviours, whether you are aware or not. My teenagers, for example, observe my driving style, my attitude, my energy, my approach to challenges and they learn. We, as parents, leaders and professionals, model behaviour and practices that influence others. At the core are integrity and congruency. Walking the talk is crucial if we are to influence people in life and work.

Networking is more like 'farming' and not 'hunting'

The truth is that when you need a network, it's too late to build it, my friend. If you think networking is a cheap, sleazy sales technique, I'm here to tell you that it's not. I see networking as a natural way to establish human relationships in special circles where people of similar interests come together. That's why I see it more like farming, planting the seeds of good quality relationships that will last a long time. Not a quick exchange of profit or business, or access to information. Therefore, I see my network as a great quality group of people to whom I add value, before I even request any favour or help.

My network is wide and high. What do I mean by that? Wise networking is done horizontally (among peers and colleagues in the same industry and at the same level) plus vertically (levels above and below your range of influence and role). I learned this years ago. At the beginning of my career, I used to attend tech events and, as one of the only women at those conferences, all attendees were often welcomed with a line that started like this: "Welcome to all the engineers and also the nice ladies." As soon as I heard that, I knew I was in one of those boys' clubs. At first, I felt awkward. I definitely didn't feel like 'networking' with everyone, and if I did, I'd talk to anyone who happened to be at the same table during coffee breaks.

During a conference in Helsinki, I met Kimberly. A black powerhouse lady, C-suite level player in an American tech company. She was approachable, a natural connector, and an outstanding listener. As we talked, I felt as if I was the most relevant person in the room in spite of being in a busy hall. It was her incredible capacity to focus and have a meaningful conversation. She advised me: "Network always up and to the sides." She meant, the best is to connect with people up your level and horizontally within your matrix. It's not vertically *or* horizontally, effective networking aims at *both* directions.

She suggested I look into my network and spot someone who was above my salary by two levels at least, a person who it would be great if they knew my name and face. I later understood that establishing powerful and solid networks is a valuable cornerstone in anybody's career.

How is your network today? When you look at your directory of contacts, are they on the same level as you? Who should know your name and face and the value you add?

Now, successful people who value networking are all about adding value and giving. Unsuccessful people that misuse their networks are always thinking *what's in it for me?* My mentor, Gudrun, showed me some important strategies that have served me well. I want you to have the valuable network that benefits from having you around, and also that can support you in your career when you need it. Interested? I now go around the world giving talks and training solutions for women on effective networking practices.

Recently my coachee, Arianna in Milan, wrote to me, letting me know she's finally part of the editorial board she had long wanted to belong to. She signed off with: 'The *farming* (networking) tips you gave me worked out!' I'm so glad when I get news like that. I'd like you to have these networking golden nuggets for your next conference, congress and networking opportunities.

Do your homework before the event

Know who'll be there, who's hosting and what common interests the people in such settings share. Be ready to contribute and provide value whenever possible.

Introvert? No problem

If you are naturally an introvert, here are some tips that can help.

Firstly, you don't really have to meet more than one person or group at an event. Introverts' energy is depleted when they feel they need to interact with large groups for a long period of time. You don't have to. You can, in fact, network with a very small group for the entire event and have a sense that you had a meaningful conversation.

Secondly, you don't have to talk the entire time; in fact, the best people who master these skills ask interesting and powerful questions that elicit good conversations. Go and find your one or two jewels in the crowd.

One more thing, if you are an introvert, you want to get there early and become integrated into the first part of the event in a small group, rather than getting there late when it's harder to interact with well-established groups.

Now, here is the trick. Most conferences will schedule coffee and drinks breaks, right? What do most women do during that golden 15-minute break? You guessed! Stand in the ladies' room line waiting their turn. Unless your ideal network contacts are also there, you want to use your golden minutes wisely. Either leave five minutes prior to the break and take care of any bio-stop you need, or do it later. The idea is that when the break starts, you are available to spot people you are interested in establishing contact with. Again, be smart and strategic. If you are like me, we are busy women, so we want to be selective and use our time wisely. Never underestimate the power of establishing contact with the organisers and hosts. They can tell you more about the attendees, and if done well, you can also request a quick introduction to someone you want to meet.

Be ready to connect and contribute

You decided to attend a networking event, so make sure your method of connecting with people is clear and at hand. Please avoid writing your coordinates on napkins and slips of paper. Have a professional card that says you take yourself seriously, or an easy to connect way that also speaks of your presence and your personal brand.

The spotlight effect

Successful people who connect efficiently use their spotlight effect wisely. It's as if the spotlight on the stage shines on someone. Ideally, you don't make it shine on you 100% of the time. You share the spotlight. You connect with people with an attitude that says 'here, you are!' instead of 'here I am!' In other words, it's about being interested and not only being interesting.

Good conversations start with good listeners

Have you ever talked to someone who speaks while looking at the ceiling, making practically no eye contact and having a monologue? How's that like? Awkward, right? Well, make sure it's not you who is talking like that. Talk, and when listening, give signs of acknowledgement that say 'I follow your thoughts, I see, I hear you'. Having a good conversation is like a tennis game, the ball goes and comes back; the conversation flows at both ends. When you are able to listen and acknowledge, you understand, ask relevant questions, show interest, you show you care. A good listener in the room is like a precious gem.

A short kick-ass elevator pitch

I train people worldwide to pitch and sell their ideas. We all sell something. Perhaps your company is selling products or services and perhaps you need to sell the idea of a new research project to a stakeholder. A short and effective way to express and sell an idea is an elevator pitch. It's called like that because you should imagine that you're sharing an elevator (lift) with a stakeholder, potential investor or customer, and need to get their attention and interest in the brief time it takes to reach the top floor.

People's short attention span makes this an essential skill. I often coach engineers who attend the most important fairs/tech-expos in Europe. They are all looking for possible partners and investors. I usually teach a few methods to pitch good ideas. I want to have the most straightforward model, and for now, it's called the 'Speedy Pitch'. It's a concise model, it's short and to the point. It has three elements. Whenever you need to explain what you do, keep in mind the answer that it's not really about you as a person; it's about the **value** you add to the people that work with you.

I suggest you create yours, it's simple: when you are asked '*What do you do?*' you may say '*I help* (who do you help?) *by doing* (how do you help them?) *so that* (why is this important or a result?)'

Example: a headhunter may say: '*I help tech companies find the best young talent in the digital market. I do this using the power of social media channels to attract top talented engineers. The companies end up with quality people to innovate and young people find a place to grow.*'

How does yours sound? Remember it's juicy enough to express what you do, and also short enough that anyone can understand and remember it. It elicits more conversation, it engages others. You can also add an exciting piece of information, an intriguing fact or interesting statistic and make it more relevant, and easy to remember.

Catch the attention of goldfish – short attention span

We live in the short attention span world. Our smart devices have helped us drop our attention span to only a few seconds. There's a saying that, nowadays, a goldfish may have a longer attention span than people while surrounded by social media and tech devices. So, if we know it only takes a few seconds to make a good first impression, this piece of information is relevant. Let's see, imagine your ideal high-ranking stakeholder is right in front of you. You have a few moments to make your point. You are competing with interruptions, short attention span and other people who also want to talk to her/him. Use proactive, clear language. Keep your message simple and short. Make your point in no more than three important chunks of information.

Be memorable

Yes, your personal brand has a special individual flavour. There's something that stands out about you, I'm sure. There are things like height, dress or hairstyle, your smile, your business card, something you did or said, your energy. Something. Build on that. The idea is to be memorable. Why? People will recall you more easily, associate you with ideas and possible projects and the collaboration you are looking for. You effortlessly come to mind, what you do and what recommends you.

Personally, I add a bit of humour when I introduce myself, about the paradox of being Latin yet having the most common Swiss-German surname, or coming from a *small* town, Mexico City. People smile and remember the word games and contrary ideas – and me! So I've had people who then Google me years after we've interacted because of something I mentioned or my surname and Latin background. Things that are easy to remember. Don't shy away from wearing colour in business casual or business smart that suits you well and you feel good in. Colours, outfits, and aspects that make it easy for people to remember you help them remember your value too.

Wow! So many strategies you can choose. Keep your big goals in mind. Again, focus on what you want to achieve, the results and impact you wish to have. Then select the strategies you want to try out first. Adapt them wisely. Remember you can only grow if you are willing to feel awkward and a bit or very uncomfortable when you try new things.

In the chapters that follow, you'll see how you can influence your results by getting the support you need. How to persuade and convince even the most demanding player in your workplace. And how to advance your ideas and your results. Keep reading.

Leverage your network

It's about a *quid pro quo* effect. Many women I train in networking skills admit to being uncomfortable talking about this, except it happens all the time. So, we deconstruct it better and work out how to use it to our advantage, considering the benefits of the people in our network. In Latin, the expression means 'something for something'. I'm not talking about simply doing things for others and expecting something in return. I'm talking about a certain level of reciprocity among your contacts and people in your network, when either you or someone else requests a favour or to take a particular action. As long as this exchange of benefits is within a legal and ethical frame, you can use the *quid pro quo* to get what you need.

My argument is that you should use it. I've seen how women tend to add tons of value to their stakeholders (information, access, knowledge and even resources) and then shy away from asking a simple favour from the very same people. When and if you've added value to your network and contacts in the past, you absolutely have the right to request help or support from them. You don't need to be afraid of sounding weak or wrong; again, when it's about something ethically OK, go for it.

Key points Chapter 3

- Key moments call for key communication skills. The *three Cs of communication:* concise, concrete and clarity. No matter how much knowledge and expertise you've got, if you are not able to express it in key moments you'll sabotage your outcomes.

- There are words that will make a difference on your career, such as *strategy*. Use it wisely in all its variations, it'll work its magic.

- You've learned tips that will make everyone in the room put down their phones when you speak.

- Develop a sense of gravitas and learn to hold the floor with muscular language. Express those innovative ideas with confidence and make body language your superpower. It counts for over 90% of the effectiveness in communication.

- When you need a network, it's too late to build it, so learn to network wisely. You learned tips for intro/extroverts. You've learned to leverage your network, use a *quid pro quo* effect. It's OK.

- You can gain influence over people who don't report to you and get what you want and need. Influence has a healthy mix of four elements: Delivery – Emotion – Expertise – Power.

4.

DON'TS AND THINGS THAT CAN SABOTAGE YOUR SUCCESS

"Not taking failures personally allows us to recover — and even to thrive."

SHERYL SANDBERG,
BUSINESS LEADER, PHILANTHROPIST, COO FACEBOOK

Don't compete with your message

If you are sitting in a meeting wearing and playing with a super big piece of jewellery, fidgeting or similar distracting things, I can't focus while I try to listen to you. If you are in a meeting and you are wearing a super short mini skirt – the kind of skirt great for an afternoon at the beach in Mallorca – then I would find myself distracted, and not only me as a woman, your peers may do too. If you are in front of me wearing makeup or the outfit more appropriate for a gala night out whilst explaining the milestones of your fantastic technology launch project to me, I'll have trouble following you.

I once coached a great Russian female IT specialist on being taken seriously. A minor adjustment in her wardrobe and speaking up during meetings paid off in her career.

There's nothing better than feeling great in our own skin. My recommendation is to find something that allows you to feel comfortable, authentic and is appropriate to the context in which you work. A good rule of thumb: when the lift door opens and you come out, if you look like *Friday night* and everyone else looks like *Monday morning*, you may be in the wrong film. You want to make sure you are in the right film.

I've found that certain industries are more relaxed when it comes to outfits than others. You want to adapt smartly. The culture of the organisation is an element you want to take into account.

Don't talk faster than light!

Speaking quickly, whether in your mother tongue or one of your languages, also comes with a price. Your key message is not coming across clearly. And what's worse, your ideas are coming across as unimportant sentences which are hard to follow. Some people think that speaking fast is being more effective. No, it's not. It makes you sound nervous and less experienced. Slow down and pause.

I am a Toastmaster. What is that? Toastmasters is a worldwide non-profit club that empowers people using rhetoric and public speaking skills. When I first started as a Toastmaster member, I used to speak very quickly in an attempt to deliver information fast. I wasn't aware I was damaging my presence and killing my ideas. Here's a Toastmaster recommendation: an effective speaking rate is about 120-160 words per minute. Now I personally find that while speaking to multicultural crowds where English is not their primary mother tongue, you want to slow down even more, around 100-120 words per minute. Want to improve your speaking and rhetoric skills? Check out your local Toastmasters club.

Do not use words that sabotage your success

The words you use can make the difference between good leadership and bad leadership. Good leaders know how to motivate and inspire; bad leaders seem to excel at criticism and negativity.

When we use words that are passive or weak, our own perception of the situation tends to be more negative, our listeners will sense that too. On the other hand, active, powerful and dynamic words will help us be perceived as being more capable in any situation and this impacts on our results. Semantics have an underestimated power.

Some important keywords simply sabotage our success before we even start demonstrating our work or presence. When they pop up too often in our speech, these words diminish the perception of competence, they make us sound insecure and disempowered.

Do or do not, there is no Try - Yoda

The difference between 'I will try to deliver the results tomorrow afternoon' and 'I will deliver the results tomorrow afternoon' is a clear gap in the level of commitment. This simple step shows true dedication. If J F Kennedy had said 'We will try to go to the moon... ' he (we) would probably still be trying. Solution: use 'will' or another useful option is 'intend'. Notice the difference between 'We hope to sign that big contract tomorrow...' (this sentence leaves room for doubt) v 'We intend to sign that big contract tomorrow' (this phrase expresses a more direct, proactive action).

Leave your 'sorry-ness' behind

This word, when overused, can kill the perception of personal power. And I know in many cultures it's associated with being polite and kind. Think again. When you overuse it without meaning it, the word loses its power. Before you think the word sorry is particularly necessary to offer an apology, let me share why it can sabotage someone's success.

Being over apologetic makes us seem less confident and even less competent, which can easily lead people to start taking advantage of, or distrusting us. If you say 'sorry... sorry' for things you are not responsible for, or things which are outside your control and not your fault, then you are simply sabotaging your own performance. It damages the perception of your promise of value, and it conveys a lack of confidence. Unluckily statistics show that women use the word sorry four times more than men in the workplace. Constantly saying 'I'm sorry' or giving unwarranted apologies not only prolongs your speech, it also detracts from the focus and clarity of your message and dilutes the power of the words. After a while, you may come across as untrue or superficial.

My friend Brenda, who leads a molecular research lab to treat cancer, is as smart as they come. Her British accent is elegant and her pace is calm. She only needed to work on removing the 'sorry-ness' out of her life, at least at the lab she was leading. She asked me for support, and after a few coaching sessions she eliminated these useless habits. As a result, she's increased the perception of her personal and hierarchical power. She managed to speak as the leader of the lab, as a contributor whose opinion her people would respect. It's not that she never repeated the word, though preventing it from popping out every second sentence made a huge difference.

If, until now, you've been over apologetic, you may be thinking *OK though what about other important stuff I feel sorry for – can I apologise?* Let me help you on this step. There are some things that I will advise you **not** to feel sorry about. You don't need to offer apologies for asking a question, ordering food, expressing an idea, needing time for yourself, other people's reactions or feelings, not reacting immediately to people's requests or emails/calls and stuff you can't control.

Should you really owe an apology to someone, then the alternative is a sincere, genuine way of saying 'I offer my apologies for XYZ, it won't happen again' or 'Please accept my apology'. It's much better and it shows you are taking responsibility and offering an apology in a sincere, yet confident way.

Other credibility killers and how to get rid of them

Some words kill your credibility and executive presence faster than a speeding bullet. When you use them, you're putting yourself at a disadvantage. Watch out for these and avoid them as much as possible.

Honestly – the Pinocchio syndrome

You may be using this word to add sincerity to your point; the problem is that the receiver may perceive you hadn't been honest with the rest of your thoughts or words before that moment. Weird. Avoid it.

Solution: use 'I' statements where you take ownership of your thoughts and actions.

Just – the *chiquito*-effect

Just is a 'smaller something' sound, *chiquito,* smaller in importance and substance. Every 'just' you use minimises the importance and power of your idea. Adriana, an IT specialist, would present her ideas in this manner: "I know I'm *just* a junior programmer, but I think we should do it this way." Ouch! 'Just' makes you sound apologetic or aggressive, depending on your intonation.

Skip the word. That's it. Have a mental shift from 'my ideas are not that important' to 'my ideas matter'.

Unnecessary disclaimers

These are sentences you add before you present your big idea or suggestion, sounding like this: 'I'm no expert, but…' or 'I'm not sure what you think, but…'.

I have been guilty of using phrases like those in the past. I had golden ideas, though I announced them with a self-deprecating phrase, intending to sound humble or not too selfish or important. No wonder others ignored my ideas at first. I discovered that if I wasn't proud of my ideas, why should anyone else buy them?

Solution: I started to trust in the value I had to add, I eliminated unnecessary warnings and disclaimers. I started speaking up, no disclaimers or apologies. People listened. It works. I suggest you throw your ideas out there. Let your stakeholders decide what they think of them. Don't sabotage them before you let them out.

'I can't'

Imagine this: 'Adriana, can you send me the report today?' Adriana: '*No, I can't because the numbers are not yet confirmed by my R&D team and it's just, like, risky to send it today.*' WHAT? Adriana has obviously not read this book. When I say 'I can't' I am expressing 'I don't have control over my actions, ability or ownership'. When you say 'I can't' it sounds like you lack the skill to do something. It's a little thing, though 'I can't' limits you and shapes the way you are perceived.

Solution: use more frank and direct expressions: 'I won't'. This is a skill that can be hard or intimidating to adopt at first, though it's very useful, especially if you are dealing with people who step on your boundaries and order you around. Example: '*I won't send it before the R&D team confirms the numbers*' or '*I will send them as soon as the R&D team, etc.*'. Don't forget to inject a positive attitude and confident body language.

Stop 'umming...'

Umm, well… like… The habit of adding markers and fillers when speaking, my friend, is the credibility killer number one. Fillers are completely unnecessary words, they add no value whatsoever to your messages, and even worse, they make you sound insecure and doubtful. They are proportionally opposite to the perception of the credibility I know you want to express. The more 'umming' you include in your speech, the less you will be perceived as a credible contributor, presenter or professional.

Solution: pause and don't use a filler or marker. Instead of saying 'She was, like, so happy!' say 'She was very happy!' Practise.

Consciously listen to your 'likes' and 'uhmmms'. Notice how people around you use these words, that will also help raise awareness of this killer habit.

You also want to record yourself talking, for example, on the phone. Afterwards listen to the recording and spot your filler sounds. This is a good first step to developing awareness and finally eliminating them.

Kick the 'but' out of your life

My client Anja, a German scientist working on immunology, used to experience much more resistance in her workplace than she does now. Sentences like: "David, I'd really like to help you organise that clinical trial, *but* I am behind with other stuff!" would backfire. Every time she used 'but', any nice, warm intention she had expressed before that word was practically forgotten. 'But' creates conflicts and barriers in communication. Are you experiencing resistance from your teams or stakeholders? It might be because there are 'buts' preventing the flow of communication.

Solution: swap it for *and* or *nothing*. Yes, to link two sentences with *and* is much better. Either version of the sentence could be used, it's a matter of getting organised and creating options. Or you could stop. Silence. A pause in between. Then the second sentence. This lets the person know the two thoughts are two different parts and can be dealt with separately. Use the autocorrect function on your word processor and email program. Really. Do it. See how you'll reduce resistance in life and get more buy-in. Be gentle with yourself when working on the elimination of these killer habits. Don't beat yourself up every time a disclaimer or uhmm pops up. Only notice it. Take your time. Slow down and do it again when you have a chance and you'll get it.

Pitfalls on networking

When it comes to making a wrong move in networking, there are several, and I decided to pick three sentences that immediately turn me off when I hear them.

First: 'Can I pick your brain about XYZ?' Nope. You can't. This sentence makes anyone sound needy and selfish. Especially when that person hasn't invested anything in developing a relationship.

Another example: 'Can you introduce me to XZY person in your company or network?' Again, without having built a relationship and a reputation, no one should be asking to be introduced like this at an early stage.

And finally... ta dah... the worst question to ask during a networking first-time conversation is: 'Are you hiring?' This is a big ask on a first chat. Let's be givers and not takers. Build relationships, invest, add value and then/when/if the time feels right, you can tap into the power of your network while you continue to add value.

Key points Chapter 4

- In order to be successful from here on as a STEM woman, know that unlearning obsolete beliefs is as important as learning new methods that serve you. That'll be the new You 4.0.

- This chapter shows you why and how to remove old socialisations, ideas and habits that may have been sabotaging your success.

- Now you know that some communication habits are in your way between you and what you want to achieve. From being over apologetic, to saying useless words such as *just, maybe, like, but, try* or using the uptalk when attempting to make statements? Time to stop.

- Trust yourself. End your sentences with a full stop, confidence and the absolute belief you deserve to be there.

- When you don't ask for what you want or need, when you fail to say no to an unreasonable request, you aren't gaining influence or power. When you doubt yourself and poll for approval before making a decision rather than taking a stand, you are sabotaging your success. Full stop.

- I know you can overcome those limiting habits and the time is now.

5.
GREAT THINGS NEVER CAME FROM COMFORT ZONES - TAKE RISKS

"Science doesn't exclude gender or any other characteristic. Science requires all the talent of women we can get."

SILVIA TORRES-PEIMBERT, MEXICAN ASTRONOMER,
PRESIDENT OF THE INTERNATIONAL ASTRONOMICAL UNION

Great things never come from staying in your comfort zone. Which idea or feeling comes to mind when you say the word risk? Are you thrilled or excited? Or cautious and averse to it? The way you perceive risk will depend partly on your past, your upbringing and there's a socio-cultural layer to it too. Smart women are self-updating. Regardless of what shaped your idea of taking risks, rethink it, it's worthwhile. I know you are serious about getting to your next level and it's going to require taking risks.

Don't avoid your fear, instead dance with it

Not only do I come from a large Mexican family, I'm also the proud granddaughter and daughter of two extraordinary women, warriors in their way, who raised their families as the only breadwinners. They taught my sisters and me that fear is part of life, and I'm the driver of my life. My grandmother, a survivor of the Mexican Revolution, used to use analogies. "Dance with the fear, *mi niña* (my child) because it's not going anywhere." So I learned how to 'dance' with it every time it pops up. She was so right. As I travel the world as the very first person in my family to leave Mexico and reach all five continents, her words are always with me. When I feel that fear crawling up and wanting to paralyse me, I remember her. I want to show how this can work for you.

Fear may pop up when you spot chances to grow, new positions, a challenging promotion, or an opportunity to meet someone you want to ask for mentorship. Chances are you don't feel 100% ready, though deep down you know it's the moment to do it! Don't wait for your mind to talk you out of it. Don't over think. If you expect all the chips to be in the right place, you won't do it. The perfect moment may never come. The perfect moment is *now*.

It's time for you to face your fear and acknowledge it. Don't even waste time trying to 'delete it'. It's not going away, and it has a reason to be there. It's part of your warning system, though know it's not a compass to set the direction. Challenge your fears, look them in the face.

Toddlers and psychopaths

In my view, those two groups of people are completely fearless. Whoever says that attempting something meaningful and challenging has never made them feel afraid is probably lying. We are all afraid of something. So I don't suggest being absolutely fearless, certainly not. I'm saying do it, not fearlessly but in spite of fear. Do it with the one and only thing that we all need to expand and grow: courage.

Take Leah, a 33-year-old postdoctoral researcher in the Netherlands. She propelled her career forward when she took the risk of presenting herself and her research on endocrine cancer before feeling 'fully ready'. It was a risk; she wanted to convince people of the potential and not only based on her own experience. Most people waited longer and published more papers before attempting to move further along. She wanted to speed things up in her career, so she approached an experienced professor with similar research interests in the USA. That meant taking a chance to ask for collaboration and endorsement. She went on to apply for an extraordinary grant from a Dutch organisation for scientific research and she got it! It meant she could start her postdoc at the lab of her most ambitious dreams at the right time. Now, looking back, she knows if she had waited to be 'fully ready', her career advancement would have been slower, and her research delayed.

Here's what I know. Women are natural connectors and many experience an inherent discomfort about risks. Many of us see cool social media posts saying things like 'trust yourself', 'go for it'. Well, I know thinking about confidence doesn't give us more confidence. Building new brain pathways and taking action does. We need to take more risks, more often, to rewire our brain to take more risks. That's it. The willingness to attempt it and actually do it.

If you are still risk averse, park the emotion you attach to risk. Ask for what you want. Identify the gaps, negotiate wisely, upscale accordingly. All these steps will require you to take risks. It's natural to be more risk averse when there is something more important at stake. I get it. It's scary to put yourself and your work out there and know that it could blow back in your face. Though when you are committed to making a difference, you can't play safe within the lines all the time.

Today, STEM fields are areas that are very competitive and where brilliant minds shine. However, a guaranteed job for life is now a rare gem, and the conventional career path is no longer the norm. Doing things the way they've always been done in the past is, perhaps, the riskiest thing you can probably do today.

Have you seen the viral video of a shirtless guy at a summer music festival a few years back? (search for 'crazy guy dancing'). He was dancing on his own to his strange rhythm while the crowd around just sits and watches, it's awkward. Minutes pass by. Then something magical happens. A second guy joins him. Then another, then a few more, then in about three minutes, a crowd of several dozen rush in, and a movement starts. Here is the question: Who took the risk? Most people say guy No. 1. I say it's guy No. 2. He decides to join the strange-looking dancer and 'risks' his personal reputation, though it's only then that change happened. Sometimes it feels like that when your reputation may be on the line. Sometimes you'll feel like the first guy and at times like the second one. What counts is that decision to take action.

How to become a risk taker

Risks must be taken because the real danger in life is to risk nothing. For a brief moment, imagine yourself five years from today. Except that for this mental exercise, you will assume you didn't make any changes, you played it safe and obeyed every rule (written and unwritten) and didn't take significant risks in your career. How does life/career look like in that image? If anyone thinks trying is risky, wait until life/career change hands him/her the bill for not trying.

Where to start? Start with the little things. Take baby steps, in non-stressful situations. Get out of your comfort zone. Then endeavour to take bigger steps.

You have to be willing to fail, *chica* – it's as simple as that

Almost everyone wants to advance, to win, to get further or make an impact, but almost nobody wants to do what it takes to stand out, speak up and take risks. Be willing to put in the extra mile and take risks. I'm not saying it's easy, I'm saying it's worth it.

Leaving your comfort zone can be hard in the beginning, it can feel chaotic in the middle, and great in the end. After all, the great ideas you've got to offer in your field can find a place to shine and impact the world. Your contributions to this new 4th Industrial Revolution are way too important for you to play small. The future of the field depends on people like you, on women like you. Trust yourself and take chances. You will either find success or you will survive, that's it.

Failure is an opportunity to learn from and expand. Get good at failing. I used to believe failure was a dead-end or something to be ashamed of. I've now come to realise failure is a teacher, a detour, it's information and at times it's simply a delay. Success isn't guaranteed. A 'no' is not a rejection, it's a re-direction of my efforts. What matters is to have the ability to recover from setbacks and keep going.

Whenever I 'fail' at something I keep a record, I realise that it is not the way to do things. I keep going, this time wiser and better informed.

Pleasing people and the fear of disappointing someone

I've coached thousands of women, from the highest ranks in organisations to heads of government and including Olympians. If I had to pin down one of the main limitations that stops most people from taking a risk and makes them fear failure, it's this: the fear of doing something that may disappoint someone they care about. At times this goes back to the early years of childhood or youth. If you let your adult self get stuck with unresolved issues from the past, then your potential is locked.

Drop a few sandbags

Once I had the chance to have a conversation with Mr Bertrand Piccard, a well-known Swiss entrepreneur and pioneer. Along with Brian Jones, he was the first to complete a non-stop balloon flight around the globe. He made an interesting analogy. Just like an air balloon needs to drop sandbags to fly higher and faster, the same applies to anyone pushing boundaries and overcoming self-limiting beliefs. What are the sandbags that hold your flight low and heavy? What needs to happen so you decide to drop some sandbags? When you do, you too will move forward.

Get real about what is worth taking the chance for. Is it that promotion, that top management or C-suite level position, a salary rise, that juicy grant, that publication you want your name on, that ambitious kick-ass project you want to lead, your lab, working space and the team you want to lead? What is it? Get real. Don't fool yourself. Think big.

Write it down. If it's relevant and important, as you write it you feel a mix of excitement and nerves. Then you know you're up to your boldest goals.

Ditch impostor syndrome

My first work trip was to New York and Washington DC. I had been freshly hired by a big blue-chip company, and my boss thought I was the right person to take a new IT sales program. I remember entering the room and immediately felt like I didn't belong. As if my new peers were soon going to discover I was a fraud. As it turned out, at the end of two weeks, it was clear I was the right person on the team to take that assignment, I belonged there and I got the job done. It's interesting how our mind can play tricks on us.

Have you ever experienced that? It's called impostor syndrome, or what psychologists call impostor phenomenon. It's an internal phenomenon, experienced as chronic or strong self-doubt. According to studies carried out by the Universities of Stanford and Georgia State, it's quite common. Around 70% of employees have felt at least once like a fake and fear people around them will find out they are not as talented as they think. Wow!

Next time the impostor syndrome kicks in during a meeting or presentation or anywhere, this can work:

- Ask yourself this one question: *Does this thought help me or does it get me stuck?* (you know the answer to that question). Be pragmatic.

- Remind yourself of the value you bring, over and over if necessary.

- Reach out to your 'friend's voice'. *Chica*, change the script. Think what you would tell a friend who's nervously facing a challenge. Practise self-care and treat yourself to encouragement.

Finally, if self-doubt persists, open up to people you trust and to someone who can provide you with honest constructive feedback.

It's amazing what we can do when we ditch the unrealistic expectation that we should know it all.

Timing

I ask this question to hundreds of women in my leadership workshops. When is the best time to take a risk at something? I recently asked a group of female biologists and natural science MBAs. Most women would wait for something or a trigger until they decide to take a risk. That something can be getting more information, getting the approval or consensus of a group, or when there's almost no other choice. In other words, an external factor. I'm here to suggest three things that can get you ready to take risks and when to make the best of it.

Take risks when things are going fantastically

Why? Because when you get to a level in your job that you can do it in your sleep, it's time to take a chance. Are you the expert? Great, choose your next level and take a risk. Don't get too in love with the comfortable situation you've had for a long time. Especially if you already learned everything you could in that position. That means you are in a more powerful spot to leap. You can leverage a future negotiation and step further. Do it while you're not under stress.

Take risks sooner than later

You are more ready than you think. Look, knowing is different from assuming. Aiko, a professor at a renowned Swiss engineering university, would complain that only male colleagues were given assistant professor roles. She was working as a lecturer for years before she decided to approach the Dean. She later found out that there were four times as many applications from men than from women for senior lectureships. There were also ten times as many applications from men than from women for associate professorships. Even though the promotions were awarded almost equally, the disproportion in the number of applications had an impact. She promptly made her application and got it six months later. Aiko was not fully ready in her mind, yet she had been prepared for years. When you put together information and have the courage to ask, more often than not things happen.

Take risks when your intuition talks to you

Sometimes your intuition is yelling at you or sometimes only whispering. When it comes to taking risks, my intuition is usually spot on. I call it 'my superpower'. And it's probably your superpower too if you listen to it. Whenever I've ignored my intuition, I got in trouble. When you review your list of scary, boldest goals, you want to tune into your intuition. It helps you calibrate the impact of your decision and look for potential gain. Go back and review the result of the 'compass' exercise in Chapter 1, it reveals important coordinates that can match your intuition. The problem is, at times there's too much noise in the environment, we are distracted, tangled up in 'shoulds' or 'musts'. Sometimes we can't hear it well. I started meditating a few years back, taking walks and doing things alone that got me in touch with myself. Most times, I can clearly hear it and I trust it. Mostly I can easily distinguish my tuition (inner wisdom) from my inner critic voice (my scared ego). The tunes they play are different. One looks for potential and the other comes from a fearful place.

How to crush self-doubt and boost self-confidence as a smart woman in STEM

OK, the picture is clear. Women are primarily under-represented in STEM fields overall. This persisting gender gap problem has yet another source: the pipeline problem. Women turn away from math and science in significant numbers partly because of the negative stereotypes and ideas society and industry holds. This can make them feel 'out of place' in early stages. Recently I interviewed a group of young women in Latin America who were about to decide on their study area. They said they don't feel they belong in STEM. It's a pity since we need their potential and talents. I'm determined to provide more tools and strategies to women in STEM to navigate their environment with a better chance of succeeding. I am also determined to educate organisations on how they can foster environments in which women too can flourish.

I picked six strategies that can help you crush your self-doubt and take the driver's seat in your career in any STEM field and business.

Find your two stars – mentors and sponsors

If mentors talk to you, sponsors talk about you. While mentors give, sponsors invest. Yes, find these two stars. Your first star/s is/are a mentor/s who has already done what you want to achieve. Be strategic. Be creative about your approach to them. Select a mentor who can empower you to see a possible future and believes you can achieve it. Mentorship is a two-way street. Be aware a mentor gains too. I've got many mentors. I personally admire Professor Gudrun Doll-Tepper, a professor in the field of inclusive education, physical activity at the University of Berlin and Ms Anita de Franz, American Olympic rower, member of the International Olympic Committee. My mentors not only model leadership for me and others, they often sit in my seminars and let me show them what I can do as a coach.

In academia, for example, good mentors enhance peer recognition, job satisfaction and increase their understanding of the organisation. Finally, your university, institution or company also gains. Mentorship fosters more loyalty among employees, and increases reputation to the outside world because it values its members and their growth. So, it's a win-win for everyone. Do not shy away from approaching a person you admire. Be enthusiastic and efficient in pitching the idea and plan. You'll get back as much as you put in. Although it's essential for all women to do this, in particular, it's an acceleration factor for women in STEM fields.

This is how I got a mentor

I met Manfred at the tech company I was working for in a European IT systems company. He opened up a team meeting with very inclusive language. He'd say things like 'he or she, his or her', and always refereeing in a clear, respectful manner to several cultures present at the table. I immediately noticed he was a thought leader and a role model for many in the company. I wanted to be part of a consulting team that worked closely with his business unit.

I observed him throughout a few months and made sure my work had higher visibility in his eyes. I wanted him to see my direct contribution. I made sure I didn't skip those strategic meetings and let the professional relationship evolve organically.

When a promising project came up, I asked him for a meeting and made the 'ask'. I requested him clearly to mentor me. We agreed we would meet up early before every meeting with our key client. We'd have an early coffee chat at the train station and we'd discuss who and how we would conduct parts of the meetings, and he advised me on relevant issues.

At times, he'd put more pressure on me, instead of on other people in the team, and he always checked back if it was within my possibilities to deliver. I didn't check out when I felt challenged, even though I felt like it from time to time. You see, a mentor doesn't replace your manager or boss. A good mentor will encourage you to make positive choices, promote high self-esteem, open up paths and doors if possible, support professional achievement and to help you think differently.

Do you have one? Get a mentor within or outside your company. If you ask me, this is a shortcut to success.

Get a male sponsor

As we reviewed, the numbers of senior leadership seats within STEM fields are predominantly men, so it's very likely you'll end up getting a male sponsor. This is a short story on how sponsors have created positive impact on my path.

In my career in tech and even now as a professional speaker and corporate coach, I often want and look for active sponsors of my work. Sponsors' actions often are factors that catapult someone's career and success.

In 2007, I had made several attempts to be an external coach for one of the largest pharmaceutical companies in the capital of biotech, Basel, Switzerland. I had experienced modest success. I knew I had to be more strategic, I had been wasting time talking to the wrong people. I was introduced to Olivier, a communicative and engaging personality. He was part of the executive board team. I noticed his portfolio was measured by innovation. I figured out, most good sponsors take an interest in one's career, not out of altruism or like-mindedness, but because they can benefit too. I knew he was outside my first visible circle of contacts. I directly connected to him. I wanted first to add value to the relationship.

I concretely suggested carrying out a pilot project to coach his team on creative thinking and cutting-edge innovation techniques. He loved it. After their excellent feedback, I felt I was confident to request his endorsement. He was kind and smart putting in a good word for my work within the company. His reputation was also on the line, but he knew I could deliver with a high-level solution to C-suite and senior management teams. He has recommended my work among his high-level contacts within the industry for years.

To this day, I still get stretch assignments that come from his side, and he always offers me critical feedback that I need to hear.

Looking for a sponsor can feel awkward. Make sure you first create a relationship, look for mutual ways to add value and be specific on your request.

Cultivate your tribe

It is great to have 500+ LinkedIn connections, though what's really important is to have a group of people who are truly interested in helping you reach your boldest goals. People who can have your back and with whom you develop a relationship. My network is large, though my tribe clearly consists of a smaller number of people.

The University of Cincinnati psychology programme found one of the determining factors for women who succeed in STEM fields. It is to get encouragement and support from friends, family, other researchers, and research advisors or leaders in the organisation. You need a net to help you bounce when necessary.

Ditch perfectionism

The same study found that it's often the case that women who focus on growth instead of perfectionism advance at a higher rate. In 17 years of coaching, I've seen how often 'perfectionism' can be a real showstopper and it can paralyse anyone's efforts. I coach competitive professionals, and high achievers. Many, including myself, have struggled with this devil's advocate. I decided to choose progress and growth over perfection some years ago. Be brutally honest with yourself, and answer this question: Are you a perfectionist? Don't worry, you are not alone. For now, I encourage you to start letting go; small things at first and then the more important things which you may be stuck on. I offer you another word to replace perfectionism with: *excellence*. Striving for the first is demoralising, striving for excellence is motivating. Let's be real, not perfect.

'I want to, I can, I will, I did it!'

This is the title of a three day-leadership experience, which I lead for professionals worldwide. I came up with these four steps after working for years with Olympians, actual elite athletes who win medals at the highest level of their discipline, specifically female elite athletes. A technique that is applicable to pretty much any field. I want to give it to you, in STEM fields, since you'll need it to break limits and crush self-doubt.

I see *self-confidence* as one of the most fundamental factors to be unlocked if we are to attempt and achieve great things. I'd like you to consider this: there's a general misconception that confidence is something we're born with, a personality trait. It's not, it's a skill. Like any other skill, it can be learned and improved on over time with practice, effort and repetition.

I attended the Olympic Games in Rio de Janeiro 2016, partly because of my passion for leadership in sport and also to observe many of my coachees in action. It was a fascinating experience. I watched them stand at the starting line on the track, waiting for the gun to pop and start with 100% certainty that all the necessary preparation needed had happened. Everything from their nutrition to their sleep, to their relentless training hours and their mindset, all those years. They had done their best in preparation for that moment. Bam!

Even though their bodies are ready for the adrenaline shots in their veins, they have learned to identify their body signals as readiness and excitement instead of as anxiety and fear. Research has proven that our bodies get the same signals and symptoms when we are excited and ready as when we are in fear/stress mode. It's then our job to send the right message to the brain, so it makes sense of it. So, from now on, after all the preparation, you feel the adrenaline and sweaty hands and your heart beating faster than a Formula One car, and your breath wants to leave your body. Stop. Focus on how excited you will be when you get what you want, on presenting, or excited about letting the world know about your ideas. That's it. *Excitement.*

Walk the talk

I often coach professionals before their PhD defence. A tough experience for many and for some it's a solemn ceremony. Walking with confidence and feeling empowered as you enter a room can help get all those nerves and butterflies in your stomach under control. Breathe. It starts with your body. Being able to control your body reactions, fear or self-doubt is an essential step in any stressful situation.

Let go of the emergency brake

Have you noticed that when you have a decision to make, and you first have the impulse to go, sometimes you stop yourself in the last second? A good example is when you are at a party. The DJ starts playing your favourite song; you immediately begin moving your body, you approach the dance floor, only to notice you are practically the only one there. You stop, you don't want to take the risk. Then you slowly start making your way to the side. Your brain has just pulled the emergency brake. In life, you may be pulling the emergency brake in key situations that limit career opportunities. That idea or question you wanted to ask, you held your tongue. That time you wanted to say no to something and didn't. That time your colleague made an incorrect statement during a meeting, though you decided not to rock the boat and you stayed silent. We pull the emergency brake way too often.

Brain researchers have helped clarify this process. It's proven we only have a few seconds, from the moment we feel the impulse or have an idea, until we take action, before our brain will try to stop us and get back to our comfort zone, keeping us safe and cosy. Now, you'll need to take your time, of course, getting a tattoo, accepting a marriage proposal, deciding to move to another country, reading the small print on a contract, sure. Though not in the situations I described before. Go for it, drive smartly and without the emergency brake in your hand.

How you can put it all together

- Choose a scenario in your mind. Something that is relevant to your situation today. A starting line that you want to propel yourself across. It can be a project you are about to start or present to the world. Perhaps a paper you want to get published, a promotion or position you will put your name forward for. Something you are experiencing self-doubt over whether or not you are capable.

- If you chose something where the stakes are high, you are probably now listening to your inner critic telling you something. Perhaps some self-defeating lyrics, like a broken record, words that have stopped you from doing this in the past. If this is true for you, write down the words on a piece of paper. What does your inner critic say or whisper to you? You are acknowledging your warning system. That's fine. Doing this also sends a message to your brain and your warning system that you see it, you hear it, you notice it. Then say to it: I'll do it anyway.

- Make sure you have a support network in place: people who encourage and advise you along the way.

Select three steps that need to happen, or you need to take care of, before leaping. Be pragmatic, be concrete. Put it in the calendar. Be strategic, align time, resources or people you need to mobilise, if any. Take care of yourself, do whatever you need to do to be fine, healthy, strong and rested before the big moment. You are ready. Yes, you are. It's exciting, and you're about to leap. I believe this quote is accurate: *What you want is on the other side of fear.*

Key points Chapter 5

- Only toddlers and psychopaths are fearless. Everyone else is afraid of something and has two choices: control the fear or let the fear run the show. One way to control it is learning to dance with your fears and take risks. It'll help you overcome perfectionism, fear of failure, impostor syndrome and paralysis.

- As a smart STEM woman, you'll need to reach out for support, collaboration, teamwork and buy-in from stakeholders in male-dominated environments. You can't afford to play small and doubt yourself. Your ideas are way too important for that.

- When you decide you are ready to let your inner smart woman shine and have impact, you'll discover it's time to overcome any of these three hurdles: the need to please people, the fear of disappointing someone you care about, and the crazy expectation you have to know it all and be perfect.

- In science and every other STEM field, in this rapidly changing world, there is no recipe, there is no one way to do things — there is only your way.

- You got some new tools and hacks to make your life easier and more fun along the way. Go for it!

6.
FIND YOUR TRIBE
AND STICK TO IT

*"I feel really lucky to have had a support group.
I think that's one of the things I recommend to
other women to find people that you can relate to
and know that we are trying to help make it better
for the next generation."*

PARISA TABRIZ, IRANIAN-POLISH-AMERICAN COMPUTER SECURITY EXPERT,
INFORMATION SECURITY OFFICER, GOOGLE

Your tribe can nurture friendships, and doesn't need to be made up of women, it can also consist of groups of people from different walks of life that share an interest or have shared goals. In the previous chapter, I mentioned research suggests how tremendously important this element can be to women in STEM.

Sarah, my client, was hired to lead one of the largest teams in an oil and drilling company. She's a diligent engineer and was up for the task. Over 60 men in various locations form her team. At the company, her job is making sure that the strict regulations and guidelines for exploration and exploitation of natural resources are adhered to in Europe and Asia. A big deal if you ask me. She is part of a steering committee and sits in on board meetings. She likes the responsibility level, except she is the only woman in those teams. She used to call herself the 'token' female. Sarah worked hard, even at times without breaks. She often accepted taking care of tasks that weren't part of her role, and she was even mentoring junior newcomers. Sarah often felt exhausted, and her working pace and environment drained her immune system as a consequence of the stress.

We met in Geneva for a first coaching session, and she was considering quitting her job. She is the breadwinner at home. She and her husband decided he'd be a stay-home dad to their two children, and she'd advance her career. Although he was doing an excellent job at home, she felt her job was taking its toll on the whole family. I knew she was 100% committed to her mission and I could see it was not her job or the company that was draining her energy. She could not set clear boundaries and effective work practices. She needed strategies that would allow her to deliver results without reaching burnout.

One of the first things we put in place was the activation of her tribe. If you are the only woman in the room within STEM fields or business, one of the success factors is finding your tribe. Networking is about making a healthy number of connections to get information, exchange job tips, build partnerships and add professional value. Now, finding your tribe is different. It's a community of people who understand you, are willing to support you, and vice versa. With them, you find a place you can grow, and you no longer feel lonely on your path.

Sarah found out that in her region there was a small group of joggers who'd meet up to train together once a week and include snack time together. She had given up jogging and staying healthy because of her long working hours. She joined them and made time to reconnect with her hobby and stay fit. After a while, she started to feel energised in other areas of her life too. Besides that, she found another tribe. An affinity group. Affinity groups are associations or clubs that exist to support women in their careers and mostly share safe spaces. Sarah connected with other women within the drilling industry, other female engineers, and she was thrilled. We met for a few coaching sessions before she no longer felt alone. She's still the only woman manager in her business unit, and she wants to change that by helping managers to raise awareness of the business benefits of hiring more women. For now, she's supported and energised by her tribe. She has increased her sense of self-strength and has a reasonable level of assertiveness to set and maintain boundaries. A positive aspect of having a supporting tribe is that it can have a ripple effect.

How to find your tribe or clan

Do you have yours? I hope you do. If not, what are you waiting for?

I'm pragmatic and something I'd like to give you is the ABC to achieving something. So here's the ABC to finding your tribe, *chica*:

A. Take a look at your new compass (check Chapter 1)

Have a nice coffee break with yourself and get back to what really matters to you. Your compass (Chapter 1) already reveals a lot about this step. You are looking for these indicators to find people with the same or similar sets of values, interests, needs. Your values are intangible and are inherent to you. Your core values emphasise what you stand for. When you honour your core values, they can be a unique guide to making a decision, to behave, and to take action.

I always take the chance of using a coaching tool that helps my clients raise self-awareness and pick their most important factors using a life/career compass, their core **values.** They are your foundational beliefs, ways to think and act that are more important to you than anything else. The following is an extensive list of values: www.gabrielamueller.com/tools. It is not a checklist. Values are unique to each person. They reveal who we are. I recommend you take a good look at that list and then choose your top five core values in order of importance. They are crucial indicators that can help you make future decisions. Keep those on a note, or on a visual element, close to you. It turns out that the simple act of writing them by hand somewhere helps you remember them in key decision-making moments.

B. Who do you want to dance with?

Once you are more aware of what makes you tick in life, many decisions will become easier to make. Now you are ready to define who you want in your tribe. I've come to believe there's a clan for pretty much everyone. Use your web savviness and start looking, also in your community and region. I bet there's an online community or affinity group out there with like-minded people who would be thrilled to welcome you. In case you want to start up your own supporting tribe, go ahead! A few years back I didn't find what I was looking for, and I started my own tribe. I wanted an

English-speaking group with smart, professional women who acted and thought innovatively and proactively. Self-confident women, who were supportive, no need for ego wars, and on top of that, fun people. I found them! We've been together for four years now. We became a little clan, and as I am writing these lines to you, I think of how they've got my back, and I've got theirs.

C.   Stay curious, reach out and be active

Let go of stereotypes and unconscious bias when you enter these networks. At the core, if you choose well, they can become your tribe regardless of first impressions. There are some incredible people in some of my clans that I would have perhaps not talked to if I was someone who only judges a book by its cover.

Key points Chapter 6

- Successful smart women in STEM have more often than not a group of loyal people (mostly women) who have their backs and vice versa. This chapter showed you why and how to create yours. It can be internal or external to your workplace. However, you need one.

- These are people who you are looking for: loyal and honest players who let you know what you need to hear, even if at times it's uncomfortable. People who can lift each other up.

- On the contrary, people you don't want in your tribe are: haters, backstabbers, people who whisper behind your back, those who compare their success to yours, hyper-critical and chronic complainers. If they are still hanging out with you, you can say with kindness '*hasta la vista*'.

- The oxygen in STEM fields is innovation, creativity and critical thinking. You need to be willing to attempt, fall, stand up, dust off and do it again. That's why a supporting tribe is essential on this path.

7.
POLITICS IS A GAME - LEARN THE RULES AND TEST THEIR ELASTICITY

"Above all, don't fear difficult moments.
The best comes from them."

RITA LEVI MONTALCINI, ITALIAN SCIENTIST, NOBEL PRIZE FOR MEDICINE FOR
HER WORK IN THE AREA OF NEUROBIOLOGY

After almost two decades of coaching women worldwide, I have come to the conclusion that there was a missing piece in the puzzle of leadership. A gap that leaders fill to advance and make their vision a reality. In the new era, women can find that missing link by being politically savvy and strategic. I encourage you to consider removing the dirty connotation away from the word politics if it's in your mind. Politics per se is not all bad, in fact it is the total complex of relations between people living in society. Politics exists from the family circle to parliaments, and everywhere in between.

For all the coaching and mentoring programmes and credentials we can get, a missing link can make it or break it for women on their way to becoming leaders and furthering their careers. Women who can learn to navigate the complex world of politics will add this missing piece to the puzzle.

When it comes to rules, I'd like you to remember these golden nuggets:

- Know the rules, make sure you also know the exceptions.

- You and your ideas are here to change the world, not tied to obeying regulations.

- Sometimes you'll break a rule and sometimes you'll simply test its elasticity. This helps re-shape old rules as well.

- Sometimes, there are no rules. Then there's a chance for you to make your own.

- Lastly, when a door doesn't open, pull out a pen, draw a door, open it up and come in. You can create your own opportunities.

Politics in STEM fields

Yes, we want some fair and objective criteria to measure success by some kind of key performance indicators. Though as humans, we rely on elements of culture, perception, hidden agendas, non-written rules, tradition, history, background and many more aspects in order to make decisions, express ideas and get results.

Now, I'd like to tell you that it is an individual's hard work, intelligence and skills which solely benefit her. That would be limiting. It would be naïve to advise you to ignore office politics; it's only a power game to gain undeserved attention and popularity in the workplace. It's not. Fortunately, or unfortunately, it's more than that.

Sooner or later, we will all have to deal with politics in our careers. So why is it especially challenging for some STEM professionals to cope with them and handle them smartly?

It's because naturally scientific and engineering minds are used to working with clarity and precision, defined standards. STEM professionals expect to spot problems, get clear parameters, identify and find solutions. The workplace, whether it's an office or a lab, has additional, non-written rules and politics.

It's not a secret that many women see 'office politics' as dirty words and try to avoid it. Many of my coachees would turn a blind eye to politics, only to later find themselves isolated, blindsided victims of political moves and manoeuvres, passed over for promotion opportunities, rewards and recognition and ultimately, career advancement. They realise they must upgrade their original belief that their good performance is all they need. Harvard research shows that women view politics differently from men. Seven in ten women dislike even the word and the concept of it. They are more interested in 'gaining influence' than in 'gaining power'; I get it. Women don't necessarily want to be associated with 'playing politics'; many think they may be seen as too severe or even harsh if they are viewed as political. Politics exist everywhere. In schools, in sport, at home and indeed, at work.

Moving your ideas, getting to yes and getting what you want will require an upgraded version of your skills. If you're going to get something you have never achieved, you'll need to do things you've never done. So be ready to step up, manage your stakeholders wisely, otherwise they will manage you and your work.

Communication is vital on many levels in that it needs to be effective in delivering the intended results. How do you achieve this? First, you have to get the right spokesperson to give the message. Maria Luisa is a thought leader and excellent role model in the world of sport. When she stood for the presidency of the organisation she now leads, she came to me. Instead of focusing on her merits, we ran her campaign highlighting her political capital, her contribution to the organisation's bottom line, and we strategised using the tool I'm about to show you. She won her seat and is now serving her second four-year term. She's groundbreaking in her field and she's respected, not because she's a woman, but because she's a solid and humane leader who knows how to play the good kind of politics.

I love the word strategy, though the type of strategy that is easy to formulate, practical and easy to remember. So in this chapter, I'll give you some advance strategies extracted from the world of sport. Why? Simple. I work with Olympians as well as with thought leaders. Many of those are both.

I like the simplicity of drawing similarities from games and sports into what serves your STEM field.

Any office, lab or academic classroom that involves human interaction also involves people's values, needs, ambitions, insecurities, fears, wants and interests. As a result, there are politics. Now, good politics can help anyone advance ideas and an agenda in a fair and positive way. The bad type of politics, in which gossiping, backstabbing and other harmful practices are involved, creates toxicity at work. Your workplace may have both. Being smart at identifying which type you are dealing with is vital.

Power v influence

First, let's look at power. There are several types of power, though for now: hierarchical power and personal power. The first holds the potential to reward desirable behaviour or punish others. When formal, coercive power is exercised over a person or group, there is almost no alternative available to the group other than to comply.

Personal power is different, it's a source of influence. Your personal power can be seen by the way you show up in the world. True personal power is generated from within. A combination of a sense of self-worth and self-confidence. When you express it using effective communication skills it gets you results.

Influence, on the other hand, is a psychological, persuasive process that has an effect on the actions, attitudes or opinions of others and approval is voluntary. People under the influence have alternatives about accepting or complying.

Think about it. Are you influential or do you hold formal power? Or both? Are you able to influence other stakeholders? At the core of their differences lies the reason why many women would prefer influence and not power. Regardless of your preference, it's important to be politically savvy.

Tennis lessons and politics

Playing safe on the line or mastering the lines? Living in Switzerland has given me the chance to see Roger Federer up close and personal. He's not only good looking, if you ask me, he's a gentleman on the court and master of the lines. He can hit any point along the line, from any angle, as a result of lifelong training and mastering every centimetre on the court. He hasn't done it while playing safely within the boundaries. The same tip can serve you. Sometimes you'll have to test the limits of a rule or guideline to figure out how far you can go.

A mistake many women make at this point, and after reading this book you won't make anymore, is playing it too safe. It takes the shape of polling your idea before announcing it to the world. It happens when asking for permission too often because you are afraid of making mistakes. It shows up in meetings when you dismiss your idea by adding a warning or disclaimer to minimise its impact or when you are unnecessarily apologetic. Sometimes there are no rules about processes, so obeying or honouring non-existent rules just because you don't know whether they exist, or worse, you assume they exist, is playing too safe. So don't. Be ready to size up the risk, take the chance and go. Shoot and aim at the line. Should the ball to land outside of the court, two things can happen: nothing, you merely get what you want, or someone will remind you there was a line. Not to worry, learn the lesson and serve again.

Map the people at work as if in a soccer team and gain influence

Growing up in Mexico, soccer is one the natural preferences as a sport. I am a passionate soccer fan. I also coach players and trainers. One of the lessons I've learned to apply to organisational life is how any coach or captain maps out her team as well as the opponent's team. Know who's the connector, who's got the strongest kick, the defence, and the fastest player. I'd like you to use the same strategy in your career. Think of your stakeholders as members of a team. You'll be able to identify these key players:

- **Gatekeepers** These are people who hold particular power and access to information, contacts and opportunities. You want to get to know them and also know what they need and want.

- **Networkers** These are people who pretty much know everyone in the organisation, up and down, inside out. Reciprocity is essential in developing these relationships. Remember, when you need a network it's too late to build it.

- **Sponsors** These are influential people who may or may not be within the hierarchical structure of your organisation. Getting a well-known sponsor in your career is essential. A sponsor mentions your name in professional networks or circles which you may not have access to. It's not the same as a mentor. A sponsor talks about you, while a mentor talks with you and teaches you stuff. Can your sponsor be a woman? Sure. Though, with the obvious lack of representation of powerful, high-ranking women in your area, the most typical case will be to get a male sponsor.

- **Mentors** Everyone should have one. They come in all sizes, shapes, genders and some are more formal or casual in the way they can offer mentorship to you and benefit your career. In sport, even Olympians need daily practice with their personal trainers and coaches. Following this analogy, just like athletes, I've had a vast number of those. I've looked for and followed the best. I still do. They are usually experts in a specific area, well connected and at times busy stakeholders.

In your world, you have access to the best mentors you can get. You'll get out what you put into this relationship. In science, academia and business, you may need to be very clear on the fact you'd like a mentor. Mentors also gain from teaching and sharing their expertise.

For crying out loud, *chica*, none of these people are mind readers, so be outspoken and direct in addressing your needs and wants. If you'd like to get a sponsor or mentor, approach them with a clear argument as to why and how. You'll be surprised how this simple act will have a significant impact on your career.

- **The support team/entourage** In sport, you'll have supporters and the entourage team that is there through the good times and the bad. You also need them in your workplace. Don't underestimate the time and the quality of these relationships. Keeping them informed about your advancements and projects helps you walk together, having their companionship is important. Don't isolate yourself and deny their importance. It's also a mutual benefit.

- **The influencers** In sport, some players influence the game by just being around. Their leadership, presence and advice play an important role in the overall outcome. At work, it's the same thing. Some people influence your principal direct stakeholders. Who are they? What moves them and who they influence is important. This one is a tricky step, one you don't want to underestimate. I once coached a woman who took all the right steps to get elected to a board. Except she underestimated the former president, whose opinion was the final hurdle that turned the result against her. She thought he was out. Oh no, his opinion carried a weight she hadn't expected. Either win or neutralise the influencers' opinions. Be smart and think outside the box.

- **The opponent** In sport, in academia, in business, you may have opposition. The most typical mistake women tend to make here is to stay away from the opponent. Wrong. You want to get to know them better. This may require more than a simple Google search. I'm talking about investing face time and, when possible, chats that help you figure out two aspects: their less apparent strengths and weaknesses. In tennis, Federer, whose backhand is the best the sport has ever seen, uses it strategically when he knows the opponent can handle it less effectively. What this means is I'd suggest playing to your strengths and using your opposition's weaknesses. It's a strategy that when used within an ethical frame is valid. Again, if it's a game, learn the rules and play it well.

- **The amplifiers** In the sports analogy, the amplifiers are people and agents who speak about the game and promote it. They can also be media partners. In your work map and your workplace, these people are powerful players who decide who shines and who gets visibility. In academia they are board members who decide whose papers are published. In an office they are HR, communications departments and even external bodies that amplify the visibility of your work.

Beatrice, one of my coachees, leads a research department, though she expands her visibility and that of her teams by making sure the internal communications department includes a short update in the company magazine, online posts on LinkedIn, and that every critical tech outlet gets updated information about her team's projects. She could have kept her outcomes to herself. Instead, she's pulling available resources, sharing the credit and is now indirectly seen as a strategic contributor at the C-suite level. Her face was recently chosen to shine as the company's profile at a large European conference in her field. I am not saying that should be your goal, all I am saying is make sure you are on the radar of the stakeholders who can make the spotlight shine on you and your work. After all, great ideas and results have an impact when they are noticed, seen and heard by the right people. Don't play small. Go for it.

- **The energy leaks** These are players who need more support and energy from you than you gain from them. In sport it's any distraction that takes your focus away. At work they are the people who interrupt, who complain, who criticise in a draining way, the haters, the naysayers, the colleague who lacks planning skills and makes unreasonable requests at inconvenient times. The whiners, the drama queens, the constant talker, the colleague who wants to use you as a personal therapist, the blamer, the victim and the list goes on. These people suck the life right out of you.

  Unfortunately, it's not always easy to become aware and get rid of such energy vampires. Good news, it can stop here. Anything that takes up your time and energy is a waste. If you are to grow, to advance and thrive, you'll slowly and surely need to say goodbye to these people and interruptions. If you don't manage them, they'll manage your time. If you are the type of person who has a hard time saying no to these stakeholders, this can be a painful step. I know. Keep in mind your mission, your goals are bigger and more important than the brief, uncomfortable moment in which you'll kindly and firmly say no, and you'll claim your power, your time and energy. Your goals are worth it.

- **The referees** These are people or authorities you need to be aware of where it's a must to comply with legal or formal guidelines. These are the legal, formal, professional authorities in your area that set dates, deadlines and formal processes for you to adhere to. In sport, referees pull red and yellow cards when players don't comply. In your career, they can be showstoppers when you don't abide by established rules. Example: formal decision-makers who determine rules, deadlines to send applications, guidelines to apply for grants, board members who select your work and need official information. You want to comply and keep them satisfied. Nothing else.

- **Your team members and the team captain** Now, these are people who play with you directly. They are people who unequivocally impact your outcomes. These are relevant people who also have a vested interest in your results. These are people whose performance also affects you. You want to get to know them. Even go one step further. Know their strengths and weaknesses. When I work with women in an organisation, I invite them to observe the team, read their moves and understand how they tick. You can't afford to underestimate their impact.

  At the last Olympic Games, I had the chance to attend and see my coachees in action. It was thrilling to see the female Jamaican 100m relay team. Jamaica ran the fifth fastest time in history and won silver. Strategically, combining their strengths and weaknesses was a recipe for success. Choose the quickest starter for the first leg, then have reliable 200m specialists for the second and third legs, and finally, the fastest runner should take the anchor leg. At this level, it is imperative as nanoseconds make a difference. What's your team like? Whose performance affects you the most? How can you gain even more influence among your team? What would it mean if you play using strengths and weaknesses at an optimal level? The side effects of this strategy may generate massive success.

- **The crowd** At any sports event, there are people who, as spectators, observe, cheer on and support you or your opponent. In your world, the crowd includes those who ultimately get to hear about your big idea, either a consumer, the client, the receiver of the product or service and even those who, as externals, merely get to hear about your organisation and work. Even with minimal effort, you'd like to make sure they are informed as necessary. They can be either neutral, pro or against what you are doing. A coachee works with stem cell experiments in a lab. Depending on who she talks to, they can be curious or interested, or even against some of the aspects of her work. The crowd has a perspective, and if they happen to be the most powerful stakeholder, you want to be politically savvy and not ignore them.

How to play the game

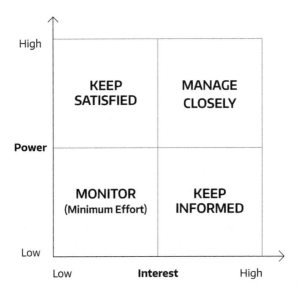

Power/Interest Grid for Stakeholder Prioritisation

Easy. The powerful and interested stakeholders get face time – meaning those who are powerful and who can create an impact on your results. At the same time, they also have/hold an essential stake in your results. In other words, when you play this game to your best ability, you'll invest anywhere from 70-80% of your time and effort, face time and build closer relationships (top right quadrant) with:

- Your team and the captain/boss decision-makers

- Sponsors and mentors

- Your opponent – if any

- Gatekeepers should know your name and your face, so should influencers

Be wise and place your amplifiers and the networkers and supporters in a relatively powerful position if it applies. They should know your name and your work. You want to keep supporters and referees informed and satisfied with less effort and more efficiency (bottom right quadrant). Be aware of some players who hold high power though low interest (top left quadrant) in your outcomes, keep them satisfied meeting deadlines, deliveries, etc. Make no mistake, they can be showstoppers if they want to.

And the energy leakers? Claim back your power, energy and time. Set healthy boundaries and honour your values. You may decide to allocate minimum effort (bottom left quadrant) or say 'hasta la vista'.

Key points Chapter 7

- Let's remove any bad or dirty connotation from the idea of politics. The only bad thing about politics is that if you don't make sure you've got a seat at the table where politics happen, then you are probably on the menu.

- Knowing the rule book is useful, though if you don't know the exceptions to the rules, or which rule you can test and re-shape, your outcomes will be limited.

- As a smart woman in STEM fields you attempt to succeed and create impact every day. You will find rejection and doors that may not open up for you. It's part of life and it's fine. When that happens, pull out a pen, draw a door, open it up and come in. You can create your own opportunities.

- In this chapter, you've learned how to map out your stakeholders according to their positions and see them as strategic pieces of a game.

- Your peers, boss, customers and all stakeholders hold different positions and power. Learning how to play and make strategic moves will help you win. Using the analogy of sports, you can now easily identify who's who and start knowing their motivators and how to gain influence in your workplace.

- They are gatekeepers, networkers, sponsors, mentors, your team or entourage, influencers, possible opponents, amplifiers, energy leaks, referees and finally your crowd or the market.

- When you identify their role, level of power v influence, you'll be able to design a mid- and long-term strategy to influence them and get better results. Keep going, you are doing great!

8.

RECOGNISE PEOPLE'S STYLES – PERSUADE AND REDUCE CONFLICT

"Science can play a leading role in connecting people because it is universal and unifying. Scientific knowledge has no passport, no gender, no race, no political party. Diversity is really a richness for humankind."

FABIOLA GIANOTTI, ITALIAN PHYSICIST, PARTICLE PHYSICIST DIRECTOR-GENERAL, THE EUROPEAN ORGANIZATION FOR NUCLEAR RESEARCH CERN

This chapter contains a simple method that will save you headaches, sweat and tears in your career. You can spot who's who in your workplace and persuade them in a positive way. Use this tool strategically to get more resources, better compensation, to be promoted and more.

Spotting your stakeholders in four typologies will make your life easier. This chapter will offer a basic understanding of the DISC model to identify the style of others and to find the best way to work with different people. It's fair to say it's a basic overview. It's not meant to replace a complete professional assessment. If you want to gain more knowledge about it or get your own, please visit www.gabrielamueller.com/assessments

It's a proven system I use and although it's more complex than the following short explanation, this piece can save you headaches and increase your chances to influence people.

Behavioural assessment and tests can be long and overwhelming, though to be fair, many are proven to be very effective. Since your stakeholders don't come with manuals and written instructions (even though that'd be cool) knowing them and identifying their traits as fast as we can pays off tremendously.

I'll use one of the most efficient models, which is the DISC Model (1928, with Mouton Marston who described people as falling mainly into four typologies). Its updated version uses names and colours such as Red in Dominance, Yellow for Influential, Green for Steady and Blue for Compliant.

Two important disclaimers about this model. First, we all have all four typologies in us. To a certain degree we have dominance, we communicate and think and act displacing behaviours that describe all four typologies, depending on the context and our role. Second, we tend to display one or two stronger typologies in the workplace. Some people have certain neutrality and display almost equally all typologies – that's possible too. We don't mean to reduce people to four colours or boxes. This is simply a model to help us identify four main types of personalities or typologies. This can give you valuable information to navigate and thrive in your workplace. This is a guideline and it's not intended to replace a professional assessment, though it can help map out certain characteristics and stakeholders. In case you are interested in your personal assessment or for your team visit the DISC section under www.gabrielamueller.com/assessments

Furthermore, you will discover six principles of persuasion. The best part is the matrix that combines it all for you with simple advice and tips to apply them as soon as possible among your stakeholders.

Red - fire: high "D" Dominance typology

Stakeholders with a high "D" typology (Dominance) will value confidence, and focus on the bottom line. As a coach in STEM areas, I often have the opportunity to persuade and influence clients with a "D" typology. One of them is Samuel, my client, a tremendously direct, blunt, strong-willed C-suite player. I knew Samuel's need for results would make him come across as driven, a self-starter and many would perceive him as extremely self-confident. I noticed how his team would often feel he'd rather fly solo instead of looking for consensus and teamwork. Samuel, and people with a high "D", hold a high sense of the value of time, so they can come across as impatient and pushy. They accept and look for challenges and are easily bored with routine tasks. They may move and drive projects quickly, so much so that they may not realise they drive solo, leaving the team behind.

As his coach, I helped him develop a bit more empathy, patience and sensitivity amongst his team. As a fast executer, he sometimes overlooks details and prefers to skip making consensus part of decision-making. Think about people like Samuel in your own working environment. How can you influence them? By knowing how they tick, what they appreciate and what they reject or avoid. The most significant fear is that others may take advantage of them or lie. No wonder they tend to micromanage others and double-check.

How you can influence a "D" stakeholder: your best strategy is to address issues directly and in a straightforward manner. I recommend sharpening your negotiating skills when it comes to setting goals and commitments. Talk to them from a position of equal power as much as possible; they'll respect your aim at being useful, direct, and focus on the target and objective.

Yellow - sunshine: high "I" Influential typology

Stakeholders with a high "I" typology (Influential and Inspirational) will be good at persuading others, like Greta, my good Italian friend, head of a task salesforce in a large pharmaceutical based in Rome. She happens to be a great speaker, inspirational thought leader and always looks like she's dressed up to impress people on the catwalk. She's charming, talkative, open, friendly, and builds relationships quickly and effectively. I bet you have stakeholders who, like Greta, are energetic, enthusiastic, their tone is convincing, and their body language is expansive. You can spot them quickly since there's something sharp and visually attractive about their persona. Often their appearance will be unique, stylish or colourful, their voice is their power, and they use it well, they'll inject humour and make the most of their storytelling abilities.

Now, all your players suffer from a fear of an intense dislike for something. Knowing what this might be is as important as knowing what they actually like. A high "I" typology dislikes being ignored or rejected. Since they are not great listeners, they tend to show impatience and have a short attention span when information doesn't involve them, something you'll notice quickly. They tend to lack the ability to follow through, active listening and may overlook details.

How to manage a high "I": persuading a persuader can be tricky. When I work with high "I", I adapt my communication style to make it easier for both of us, in a way which serves us both. I know that a high I tends to be friendly and look for recognition, I don't shy away from verbalising genuine compliments and show appreciation for her accomplishments. It's not flattery, it is genuine admiration, and it's clear and verbalised. Everyone can use some recognition, though especially someone like her, she appreciates the fact that I take the time and energy to listen to her ideas first before I suggest my own.

Think of your high "I" influential people at work. You'll increase your chances of working efficiently and influencing a high "I" typology when you recognise the social-esteem. Avoid being confrontational and make sure you don't overwhelm them with detailed information. You can, in fact, kill a meeting with such stakeholders if you show them long Excel sheets and tons of text. Instead, use attractive, visual information, easy to read – less is more – and make sure they are listened to. Make sure you allow time for them to verbalise about ideas, people and their intuition – they will often make spontaneous decisions. They cooperate efficiently if you help them meet their personal goals, so make sure they are aware of that. Lastly, don't compete for attention and the spotlight, they need it, so grant it and share it. You'll be surprised how smooth your life and work with them can be.

Green – nature: high "S" Steadiness/Social typology

A high "S" typology is the warm team member, calm, patient, a great listener and accommodating to others. This player will cooperate and offer sincere empathy, and will avoid being confrontational or questioning authority in the organisation. The harmony and wellbeing of the group is a priority. Your high "S" stakeholder will be inclusive and will attempt to build good relationships that, at times, also include partly sharing personal information. They are interested in knowing what sort of personal values you hold, as well as being interested in sharing theirs. Building trust consistently over time is of the essence to them.

Since they love stability, they'll take time to accept change. In fact, they may resist it. They'll react strongly if they feel the loss of safety and stability. So, the fewer last-minute changes you put them through, the better, they hate to be rushed. Know that they will prefer involvement in the decision-making process and prefer to work in a team role. You'll notice they then come across as humble and agreeable. This last trait decreases their ability to say no or confront others, which often causes them to feel overwhelmed with workload and multitasking.

The best way to persuade and influence a high "S" is by investing time in your meeting and face to face time. If you are coming from a high "D" (red) or "I" (yellow) your need for innovation and fast-pace results may make them feel overwhelmed. High "S" (green) may require a little more personal attention and patience. Since they base their decisions on values such as consistency, reliability and historical track records, you can use arguments that highlight your experience, time in the field, credentials and recommendations made by people they respect. You want to create a favourable environment that is personal. Be genuine and show interest in them as a person. They will be more easily persuaded when you offer clarification for tasks and answers to 'how' questions. Be patient. If your ideas are new, make sure you present them starting from current practices in a non-threatening manner; give them time to adjust. Avoid spontaneous decisions or tight deadlines.

Blue – sky: high "C" Compliant Conscientiousness typology

Take Thomas, one of my clients who is part of a team of experienced IT managers. He is kind and reserved. He deploys tech projects in EMEA regions for a large corporation. As a person with a highly blue type "C" personality according to the DISC model, he loves systems, sequences, methodologies, precise information, clarity and precision. Numbers, percentages and data sound like music to his ears. He, just like anyone with a high "C" profile, needs to work conscientiously and in a thorough way, with defined circumstances with clear boundaries and deadlines. You can spot your blue "C" typology stakeholders because they tend to use diplomacy well, they observe first then speak later. In fact, they may wait to be requested to speak, and when they do, they are tactful and systematic.

They will be looking for your expertise and value your competency and objective reasoning in your attempts to convince them. Be aware they fear criticism, especially out in the open and in public. They are self-critical about their work and sometimes spend too much time trying to make it perfect. That prevents them from delegating in a productive way and making quick decisions.

If you need to persuade someone like Thomas, in high "C" compliant typology, be aware they'll need to see facts and information to make decisions. You can attempt to keep the 'big picture' in mind, though make sure you have all the details at hand and be patient, since they'll like to see those and test the information. If there are mistakes in reports, they'll find it. Plan your meetings well, and send in an agenda before you even meet. Present your facts and arguments. Stay away from exaggerating numbers or data. Invest time in preparing; you don't want to improvise in front of a high "C". Written information, well-presented data and time to gather data and analyse it will be of essence. Keep formality and diplomacy in your repertoire, and you'll be on a high path to get their approval.

People and life offer more than four typologies, there is a vast collection of shades and colours in their typologies. **This is in no way an attempt to simplify humanity into four boxes**. My coachees take a detailed online assessment to determine their typology and personal action plan. Though since I use the DISC model for its level of accuracy and precision on the reports, this model, in a nutshell, can be useful for you. Be quick to detect your typology, and remember the other 50% of your success will depend on the way you can adapt to your stakeholders' colour and typology. It's not about forgetting your authenticity; it's about being the most effective version of yourself you can be in that particular interaction. You will remove barriers, increase chances of gaining support and buy-in, and reduce resistance. Life will be easier. That's it. I guess we can all benefit from making our lives a bit easier.

Next step is to identify your top stakeholders. The ones that ended up being highly powerful and interested in your outcomes. Now think of their possible typology, according to the descriptions I mentioned. You'll be better equipped to manage them, influence them and therefore to get what you want.

Use those new powerful X-ray glasses to determine their impact, their typology and the actions that you can take, to positively influence them. Woman, you've totally got this.

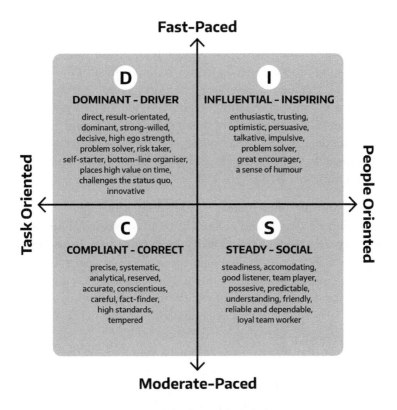

DISC Four behaviours and typologies

Key points Chapter 8

- In several STEM fields, you'll have a set of parameters and indicators to start your research and observations. Well, this past chapter was a good set of indicators that can give you the ability to identify others' communication and style preferences. It's based on a well-known system called DISC.

- Why would a smart woman in STEM want to use this tool? Because each stakeholder will have motivators, communication preferences, aspects they specially dislike or fear, all within this predictable framework. You'll have a set of special 'glasses' and power to see beyond the signals they are sending and decide a course of action.

- You'll be able to reduce tension, resistance and conflict using this tool wisely. You'll get the buy-in and green light you need for your project resources, budget and approval. Not bad, eh?

The chapter doesn't replace formal online assessments. It gives you a good idea about this tool and how to use it to your advantage. I recommend you gain even more knowledge about it by getting your personal assessment with any official DISC provider or visit: www.gabrielamueller.com/assessments to work together on this milestone.

9.
GET ANYONE TO SAY YES - CONVINCE USING THE M&M MATRIX

"I love to be a physicist, but I am also a born fighter."

PROF DR URSULA KELLER, SWISS PROFESSOR ETH AND INVENTOR OF ULTRA-FAST PULSE LASERS

Aristotle once said: "Character may almost be called the most effective means of persuasion" and I'd add your integrity and skills are the most powerful tools to persuade and influence others. You want to use them and use them wisely.

There are three top advantages you can gain when you receive more influence:

1. More trust. Your team, investors, professors, bosses and customers will feel more inspired by your trustworthiness and capacity to guide them through risk, change processes and overcoming setbacks.

2. You can become politically savvy: more influence means power. Embracing the fact that human interactions in organisations also results into politics, and understanding its dynamics can help you move important agendas forward. Whether it's a new research project, gaining a grant, publishing papers or directing a department, you'll need influence and persuasion skills. Self-promotion: leaders cut through the noise with authentic, credible self-promotion that helps others as well as themselves.

3. Concrete advancement. Yes, more compensation, more perks and better deals. When women master the art of authentic self-promotion (not bragging) and communicate their achievements, they gain more power and influence.

Now that you know more about the four fundamental typologies that can help you start understanding your stakeholders (DISC model), I want to show you the six keys to influence them all in a positive way. Why? Because I wish you to use them to get what you want and need in your career and your field.

Let's go for it. There are six principles of persuasion (so-called Cialdini principles). These are: reciprocity, commitment/consistency, social proof, authority, liking and scarcity.

When you are able to combine those with the right typology using the DISC model, what you've got is a super useful matrix to influence people around you. This is the M&M or Convince Matrix. After almost two decades of using these two models and combining them in a successful way, the M&M Mueller-Mendoza Matrix became a powerful tool that helps leaders around the world persuade others in a positive way.

The M&M Mueller-Mendoza Matrix is a tool I created that combines those 10 elements (four typologies and the six principles of persuasion). Use it to gain influence on a team, and gain support from stakeholders to work together more effectively. It can ease your path to a supervisory position, better rewards, reduce resistance and get buy-in, gain respect and be valued. Interested? I certainly hope so.

If you are concerned about being manipulative, fear not. I use this tool to help my clients to increase their power to persuade and convince their stakeholders. Be wise while using this model and combining with the M&M Matrix a bit further. When used as an influential tool and not a manipulative one, it can get you sustainable results and relationships. Manipulation involves having a hidden agenda unknown to one of the parties to its disadvantage. Manipulation is not sustainable and kills trust. Whereas persuasion is the capacity to move, motivate someone to change an opinion or perspective about something (usually presenting arguments and emotions) and the potential gains are clear for all parties.

Persuasion Principles

Six principles	What it is about	Application / example
First principle Reciprocity	Many times, we pay back what we receive from others. In other words, people repay in kind. When you offer something first, people mostly appreciate it and will make them very likely to comply with your future requests. We're deeply wired to be reciprocal.	To use this principle more effectively there are three reminders: Offer something first, be proactive. Offer something exclusive or personal. Think outside the box. People will welcome tangible and intangible benefits (not only resources, but also recognition, gratitude, access to information or places, connections, etc).
Second principle Liking	We are more likely to comply with requests made by people we like. This will pay off with stakeholders you know and also complete strangers. We often trust people who we like or are like us. Most people will appreciate feeling recognised and valued, so this principle appeals to that need.	Who do we tend to like? A few aspects can make this principle work like a gem. Similarities – people who are 'like' us (obvious similarities, physical aspect or background). Compliments – we tend to like people who give us genuine compliments. Contact and cooperation – people who support the same causes are more likely to influence each other. Identity or association – people who feel identified by the same brand, value, or philosophy, hobby or association.

Six principles	What it is about	Application / example
Third principle Social Proof	The social proof principle: many trust things and ideas that are endorsed by people they trust or are popular. Many feel influenced by a recommendation by someone they trust or admire. Many will be influenced by the consensus of the majority of a group.	The word of mouth effect is an example of this principle. The social proof principle or consensus applies especially among five groups: Experts – recommendations made by credible experts in their relevant field. Celebrities or people admired in the field – sort of the gurus of a certain field. The majority – testimonials, publications, and approval ratings. 'Wisdom of crowds' – approval from large groups of other people. When the majority of a group has adopted a way of thinking, some people will be easily influenced and convinced. Peers – people who know each other or relationships based on trust will influence in each other better and faster.

Six principles	What it is about	Application / example
Fourth principle Consistency	Many people find that once they have made up their minds they won't change it in the future. They tend to be consistent and future decisions are made to justify earlier decisions. If something or someone gains their trust over time we tend to stick to that decision in the future for all subsequent related choices.	This principle is based on loyalty and resistance to try new things and procedures every time. People who look for consistency commit to something (a statement/ stand/identity). They find rewards for investing time and effort in only one approach or strategy. If they need to change the approach they will look for historic evidence or proven records of success before they decide to change a course of action.
Fifth principle Authority	The authority principle: people tend to agree and respect authority figures, people who look/sound like authority in a field or have a platform from which to speak. Influence by authority is an incredible source of power.	The authority principle appeals to the effectiveness of symbols and platforms that people will recognise and respect, such as: Titles – positions of power/ experience. Credentials – academically recognised levels. Clothes – superficial cues that signal authority such as uniforms. Symbols – other cues that accompany authoritative roles and expertise.

Six principles	What it is about	Application / example
Sixth principle Scarcity	When something is scarce and not abundant, people are more motivated to chase it or want it. Benefits or resources that are rather exclusive, limited or special are appealing to many individuals.	This principle appeals to the need that some people have to achieve things or perks that are hard to come by. These are aspects that can make it scarce: Uniqueness – when something is considered to be one-of-a-kind. Limited-number – in short supply. Limited-time – available only during a period of time. Wanted by the competition – the fact that other people also want the same thing/ resource makes them more appealing to some people. Examples are auctions, competitions or bids.

Convince Matrix and DISC – put it all together

Imagine that you could then know your stakeholders (motivators, fears, thinking patterns and most important behaviours) and the best way to convince them and persuade them. You are about to discover tactics that combine these past two models and become a simple new tool you can use in your very next meeting or phone call. It's the M&M Matrix.

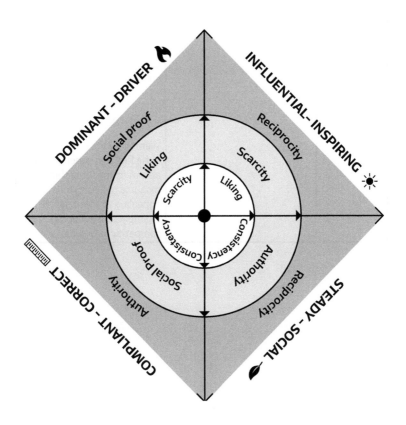

M&M Matrix visual

Influencing your red-fire/Dominant stakeholders using three principles

Your high "D" or dominant/driver stakeholders appreciate a sense of competition, determination and are self-starters and strong-willed. Understand how they tick on a good day, and also under stress. You will probably have to deal with them on bad days too. They may come across as controlling, intolerant or impatient. So using any of the other three principles, I suggest smartly, can improve your chances to get to a yes.

Applying one of the principles I suggest in the table for this sort of stakeholder will help you persuade and convince them. Their sense of ego and self-confidence will find appealing an argument or opportunity that is scarce and exclusive. Being complimented on their performance and recognised by their accomplishment is something that works well with a person in this typology. Do it in an authentic way and you will open up a door to establish better rapport. Don't use flattery, it's a chance to recognise them authentically. You can also use social proof to your advantage, especially if the references you provide are people who they admire and respect, mostly due to proven records of success, or someone who is recognised widely in a field.

How to deliver the message to a fiery red ("D" Dominant)

These are individuals who are highly sensitive to time and efficiency. Get to the point and state the aim or objective of a conversation earlier rather than later in the meeting.

You'll be able to build rapport with these stakeholders by being respectful and direct. Match their energy in subtle ways. Get to the point and use businesslike language and a practical approach. Show confidence and be concise. Your meetings will be rather brief at times so present/make your request in the first half of the meeting and be clear about what you want from them. If you disagree, make sure you express that you disagree with the facts, not the person.

You want to avoid using these principles by showing hesitation, lack of focus, rambling or putting too much attention on feelings, emotions or giving too much context. You may lose their attention or interest.

They usually will let you know if they resist your idea or deny your request. Be aware of signs such as impatience, short attention span, aggressive approach or irritability. Part of the solution to get to a common agreement will be showing willingness to take fast action, reassurance of the fact that they can control parts of the process and being kept in the loop of communication. Use arguments that can motivate stakeholders in this typology: rapid progress, improved outcomes and clear goals. Once you get their buy-in and support, be proactive on how to implement solutions and state timelines.

In order to frame your idea and utilise these principles, use words such as: challenge, results, bottom-line, forward, action, time, assertiveness, deadlines, results-oriented, objectives and goals. Describe gains, profit, purpose, determination, competitive aspects, strengths, will, speed, decision-maker, control, focus, efficacy, effectiveness, time-saving, advancement, innovation, change, evolve, autonomy.

Convince those yellow stars ("I" Influential stakeholders)

Remember these individuals are sociable, demonstrative, persuasive and communicative. They tend to be dynamic and enthusiastic sunny personalities. On a bad day they can lack attention to detail and be easily bored by monotonous communication. The three principles to persuasion I recommend using to get their support are: liking, scarcity and reciprocity in that order. Choose wisely the one your stakeholder may be more open to.

Giving genuine compliments (even in public) in an open and friendly way can be a great way to let them feel appreciated and seen. They'll tend to pay attention to their attire and appearance and would also appreciate being seen in that way too. They are also, by the way, attentive to your appearance and professional look according to the context.

The principle of scarcity applies since they also appreciate being included and taken into account, especially if the opportunity or access they are offered involves certain visibility and recognition for their work or presence. Finally, since they tend to be demonstrative and friendly, the principle of reciprocity will be useful too. This applies especially if you are the first one to offer them perks in the negotiations or as part of your ask or request.

How to deliver the message to a yellow star ("I" Influential)

When you use any of these three principles to positively influence these sunny personalities, make sure you avoid finishing their sentences or interrupting them. Do not keep the spotlight and attention on you, they'd rather be the ones who keep the attention and they'll tend to dominate the conversation. Be OK with it. Expect the conversation to be animated, at times unstructured and emotional. Avoid giving too many details (written and oral). Their listening skills aren't the best, so if you detect they are uninterested return to the point of common gain.

When you use these principles in an attempt to persuade a high "I" Influential you want to use words such as: enthusiasm, potential, vision, thrive, progress, advantages, gains, optimism, relationships, recognition, accomplishments, influence, friendliness, ready, future, spontaneity, flexibility.

Convince those Sociable/Steady stakeholders ("S" in DISC model)

Your stakeholders who are rather in this DISC typology are those who display teamwork-oriented behaviours, friendliness and have good listening skills. They need to create a sense of team spirit and appreciate safety and harmony in the group.

The three principles of persuasion that work to get their approval are: consistency or social proof, and as second and third strategies you can use the principles of authority and reciprocity.

Here is why. The principle of consistency is based on trust and it also requires time. Using this to your advantage when making a request and showing performance over time, reliability and loyalty are important convincing elements for stakeholders in "S" typology. If you decide to use the principle of social proof, you may decide to use as reference the consensus of the majority of a group as an argument. If most people/departments or most business units have adopted a policy or a viewpoint, a stakeholder with "S" typology will be more receptive to be persuaded to join in and adopt a similar view or position.

They appreciate and respect organisation hierarchies, regulations and chains of power or reporting lines. They usually avoid breaking protocols and disrupting harmonious or steady systems. Therefore, the principle of authority can be useful when presenting your arguments. This comprises backing your part of the task or negotiations with credentials, organisational charts, rules and regulations. These arguments may not influence other stakeholders as much as people in this profile.

If none of that works, you can also appeal to their sense of fairness and willingness to help and elicit teamwork. The principle of reciprocity reflects the human need for give and take in a relationship.

I don't mean to give only if you are expecting to get something in return, that isn't reciprocity, and it isn't a sustainable strategy. Use the reciprocity principle by understanding most of all to feel compelled to give something back when we receive something positive, but also, not compelled to feel indebted to others. Think about your own relationships and see that perhaps the strongest and longest lasting ones are based on the principle of reciprocity in some way or another.

How to deliver the message to a green natural ("S" Social/Steady)

You want to invest time and chit chat to create rapport. Be patient and show your willingness to take time, be cooperative and avoid rushing things in a meeting. In fact, they will often prefer settings that are not always businesslike. Perhaps a chat during a business lunch, a coffee chat at the cafeteria. Relax, and when you frame your messages and decide to use those principles of persuasion, be easy-going and don't put pressure on time or decision-making. Use the principles wisely to present benefits for both parties. Remember synergy and fairness are great motivators for these individuals.

When you present evidence use past records as part of your arguments and the principles, emphasise goodwill and consistency. You want to show you are engaged, dependable and diplomatic. They will need to feel encouraged by your interest in the group and the organisation.

You can identify resistance on their part, if they withdraw or remain silent. If they are stressed or intimidated, they may come across as impersonal or stubborn. This may happen if they are required to change processes or procedures, or if what you ask will shake the status quo. Don't despair, they simply need a bit more time to get adjusted and being asked/notified about changes and innovative ways to work. Be personal, show that you genuinely understand their position. Be sincere and empathetic.

Regardless of the principle of persuasion you may decide to use, make sure you present your ideas, new procedures or departures starting from current practices and then slowly move forward. Avoid using a quick or threatening style and give them time to adjust. It helps if you express goals clearly and their role in the overall action plan.

These few words will help you frame your request. Use them wisely to convince a high S DISC typology, they will sound like music to her/his ears: values, team, cooperation, togetherness, accomplishment, support, organisation, fundamentals, respect, goodwill, authentic, relationship, trustworthy, history, reliable, dependable, encouragement, understanding, coordination, comfortable, follow through, acceptance.

Convince blue - sky stakeholders ("C" Compliant)

Your stakeholders with this typology show orderliness, and expect and obey processes and procedures. They are motivated by efficiency and expertise. If you present your arguments and requests in an organised and precise way, you'll improve your chance to convince them. Be consistent and if you are usually a passionate speaker, you want to match their energy with a slower pace and more pauses.

The principles I suggest implementing when convincing them are: principle of consistency, social proof and authority.

The way you want to use the principle of consistency is based on historical data, proven records and evidence. Make sure you double-check the veracity and precision of your data, since a high "C" type can spot mistakes from a mile away. Allow time for them to analyse information. Listen to any piece of feedback or comment or even non-verbal cues. Those things will let you know valuable information on how to proceed. Respect their need for clarity and precision.

If you are going to appeal to the principle of social proof, be aware that they respect expertise and experience. If you mention/make citation of someone or something (studies, research, data, numbers) you want to make sure those are sources of information your stakeholder holds in a high value and admiration, otherwise you may have just missed your chance to convince. Finally, the authority principle also works because of the level of correctness and compliance of a high "C".

One of the challenges is to know when your stakeholder in high "C" cool blue is resistant or not buying your arguments. They tend to say little and if they are sceptical they don't show it too much. Be aware of body language cues that may express disbelief or input they may be withholding. If arguments are not well presented or tasks thoroughly done, they will tend to resist. Avoid being casual when presenting your reasoning. Use written and clear information. Take preparation steps before meetings (send suggested agenda before meetings and calls, gather details before discussions, analyse information before face to face meetings). Don't keep changing parameters or criteria in a request or negotiation, otherwise they will simply shut down or dismiss your request.

Now you know how to gain points: be super prepared, organised, and punctual in your meeting and in your deliverables. When speaking, offer to follow up in writing, use open-ended questions to gather information, and focus on the task and accuracy. Finally give them time to think and make decisions.

When you frame your messages, you can use some of these words to speak cool blue: task, information, precision, system, analysis, sequence, organisation, evidence, tests, results, observation, clarity, requirements, straightforward, privacy, security, reassurance, details, facts, comparison, and feasibility.

M&M Matrix

Typologies	Dominance	Influential	Social	Compliant
Principle to apply	Scarcity Liking Social proof	Liking Scarcity Reciprocity	Consistency / Authority Reciprocity or Social proof	Consistency Social Proof Authority

M&M Mueller–Mendoza Matrix

Use it to positively influence each stakeholder according to the right personality type.

Notice the four typologies and each of them will be more receptive to at least two to three principles of persuasion. It's sort of a shortcut you can decide to take to get to a yes with your stakeholders.

Key points Chapter 9

- Authority is a type of power, it gives the right to give orders, write rule books and make decisions, it's mostly given by a formal hierarchical structure. Influence on the other hand is the ability to effect ideas and actions. Influence is key for you to successfully achieve what you want. Influence is an ability.

- Your influence 'muscle' goes to work when you need to gain approval from people that don't report to you, stakeholders who don't know you yet, those who can oppose your goals, or people whose support you need to propel your ideas and projects.

- You need a tool to do this. It's the M&M Mueller-Mendoza Matrix. It's a tool that combines six principles of persuasion with the four DISC typologies (we reviewed DISC personality types or typologies) in the last chapter. It is a unique effective model that can help you get to a yes in almost every situation involving you and your stakeholders.

- The three outcomes of you gaining more influence are: more trust among your stakeholders, you'll be politically savvy, and you'll get concrete advancement as a smart woman in STEM.

- Warning: side effects may include massive success and incredible results. Be aware!

10.
NEGOTIATE LIKE A PRO - HAVE BIG AMBITIONS

"I'd love to go to space. I would love to peek out a giant window and look back at the blue marble. There's no question; I'd love to do that."

GWYNNE SHOTWELL, AMERICAN MECHANICAL ENGINEER AND
MATHEMATICIAN, PRESIDENT AND COO OF SPACEX, THE COMPANY
THAT PLANS TO BRING PEOPLE TO MARS

For once and for all let's disconnect the meaning of 'ambition' from selfishness and manipulation of others. The ability to admit our ambition is related to whether or not we think we'll be able to achieve our goals and rewards.

I know, public perception of ambitious women doesn't help much. Here's the thing: we women have greater opportunities for shaping and chasing our ambitious goals now than at any time in history. Ambition has many faces, and is not only about wealth, it can be recognition, public success, power, access to resources, etc. If you are an ambitious woman, the best is to admit it and embrace it, *chica*.

Set goals out loud and go after them without feeling guilty or selfish. So get a piece of paper and write down your highest ambitions. Read the next strategies about how to take action. I challenge you to do something about your boldest ambition right after this chapter.

Starting low has a lifelong impact

After only one year out of college, women are already paid significantly less than men. Research shows that this gap starts increasing right from those early working years. Recent gender gap reports indicate that in many advanced countries in the world (including Switzerland where I am as I type these lines), women who work full time take home 80 cents for every Swiss Franc/Dollar/Euro (or equivalent) compared to a full-time male worker. In fact, the less transparency there is around pay-parameters, the worse women do. In most countries, the pay gap is higher at the top of the pay scale. These salaries have to be negotiated and, usually, there's secrecy around pay levels. Think about the gaps that add up during our lifetime. If you learn to negotiate effectively, you increase your potential to earn a higher salary, get better benefit packages; you'll be better prepared to pay off loans. You'll also acquire all the things and experiences you want for yourself, and be better off saving for retirement. So, it's a smart business decision to invest in this skill, right?

There are also significant gaps in STEM fields. Eliminating that global pay gap is something we all can help to eradicate.

Two opposing views

About a decade ago, studies suggested that the pay gap came from the fact that 'women just didn't ask for more' and HR specialists and managers wondered and explored reasons why. More recent Harvard research suggests women experience a 'backlash' effect once they ask for more money and bigger rewards. Well, I've seen both. I've seen fewer women than men approaching decision-makers, HR or boards to nominate themselves for high-ranking positions or a rise in certain sectors. I've also seen women who experienced backlash when they asked for a better salary or more resources. Let's not be naïve, there's a chance that these strategies do backfire. When you know you want to open up a discussion for negotiation/a rise, outweigh the benefits v costs.

I know reducing the pay gap isn't just about giving women more training programmes, it's also about coaching leaders to acknowledge their own biases and defining transparent systems that make it challenging to hide large discrepancies.

Unconscious bias and negotiations

We are all biased in one way or another. Bias and stereotypes are in the eye of the beholder. The firewalls we can use to defeat bias are: facts and our willingness to challenge our bias as often as possible.

For instance, if you're interacting with a woman in the workplace and you or anyone thinks she's coming off as too touchy or arrogant, switch her in your mind for someone who doesn't look like her (perhaps a man). After doing this mental trick, ask yourself how you'd feel about that situation if it was happening with a man. Literally, *would I be having the same reaction or perception if she was a man?* You can use this to challenge your assumptions and biases about gender, age, appearances, race, etc. You will discover any difference that helps you get back to the conscious assessment of the situation. Try it out.

Unconscious bias is very hard to dislodge. I train some of the largest corporations to raise awareness and defeat unconscious bias in the workplace and in recruiting processes. We should also set up monitoring systems to ensure compensation remains broadly equal. Until that happens, unequal pay will persist.

Take Dr Low, who I met after a negotiation skills session I taught at a technology giant in Hong Kong. She approached me because she had just got what she thought could be a juicy employment offer from one of the competitors in her field. She liked her current job though, as well as her staff. She was tempted nevertheless and wanted to leverage her present contract, which had not been updated for over three years. Great, I thought.

First things first, I coached Dr Low on how to separate the issue at hand from the person on the other side of the table. Many women tend to show they feel protective and a higher level of care for the others, which often undermines their own needs when negotiating.

Next, she defined three outcomes to go after. Increase in remuneration, flexible schedule on Fridays, and within nine months she wanted to expand her team by around 10%.

Know your worth

If you don't know your own worth and value, don't expect anyone else to calculate it for you. This is a principle I coach women on. It's a combination of doing research and benchmarking, and having self-confidence about the value you add.

When I asked Dr Low to get concrete, she realised she didn't have a precise number in mind or reasons why. She found out that at the current rate, a fair increase would be more than 12%, so I suggested 15%. Why? In a negotiation, you'll need to give yourself room and flexibility, at times at least 10-20% more than you first calculated. She rated growing her team as one of her top priorities and decreased the importance of getting flexibility on Fridays; she'd be willing to wait longer for this request.

She had a picture of her wants. She had the offer from the competition. That offer carried a significant remuneration increase of 18%, zero flexibility and the chance to hire her own team after 12 months. Not bad at all. In negotiation jargon, that's called a BATNA, a *Best Alternative to a Negotiated Agreement* – a term from a classic book, *Getting to Yes*. In other words, this is the best you can get if the other party decides not to negotiate or tells you to get lost. It isn't your ideal outcome, though it's what you can achieve without their cooperation. I've even seen senior leaders going into a negotiation without knowing their BATNA and without alternatives, which is a suicide mission. Make sure you have a BATNA and research under your belt when you enter a negotiation.

Asking for too little

Women tend to ask for too little or barely enough. Find out what your 'market value' is. It'll show up as self-confidence in your negotiations. Dr Low had to do her homework and research before she was ready to negotiate. Use the web, ask colleagues, compare on forums, discreetly reach out within your network, find a benchmark. It's essential you don't guess.

Dr Low took the correct step of waiting to negotiate after she received the offer. Not before. Then she took it slowly. Timing is of the essence. She started the conversation after two coaching sessions, where she learned some basics that I want to share with you. She, like many women, was nervous about negotiating. We rehearsed this step. If you are anxious about this step, I recommend you role-play with someone you trust. Ideally, even ask your partner to 'push your buttons'. Rehearse the scenario in which you get to negotiate each aspect of the offer and also when you don't get the outcome you want. That response is one you can manage with assertiveness and grace. The 'negotiation muscle', like many other skills, is one you need to exercise before you need to use it.

It's time!

When the moment for the conversation comes, get primed. Remember the tips we reviewed on Empowering Body Language. Enter the room with a realistic mindset, but also be optimistic and adopt a positive attitude. Many people start negotiation conversations as if they are ready to sit in the dentist's chair, scared, apologetic or uncomfortable. I get it, I used to do the same. Until I got clear about the value I offer. I could then stand up for myself. You can do it too.

Build rapport and connection

Remember to go with a clear aim in mind. Use confident body language and a steady, approachable tone. Attempt to read the other person's energy and position in the negotiation. You can start by sharing a few pieces of information, having a discussion back and forth. Many women put everything they have on the table in one go, while their counterpart listens silently. Nope. It's a dialogue. Disclose, ask, validate, and choose questions that are open-ended. Then share again. Ask questions, listen more, gain more information. Information is power.

State and keep coming back to your main goals and the 'why'. When questioned, try using your value as a point of argument.

Anchoring

Our brain has something called cognitive bias that explains why we tend to rely too much on a piece of information in an offer or choice; it's the *anchor*. It can determine a starting point. Perhaps the most common question I get at this point during negotiation training is: Isn't it then better to make the first offer? Not always. Often it is better to wait for the other party to make the first move. Why? There is a risk that our anchor is way too low. That's the case in early salary negotiations amongst women. When this occurs, no wonder a low anchor usually ends in a low outcome. The decision to be first, or not, depends on the quality of information you gather beforehand. When you have enough details about your value, the market value, a strong BATNA, go first, and you won't be anchored at an undesirable point. Otherwise, you let your counterpart open up the negotiations and you need to start collecting more information. If you are anchored excessively low, my advice is simple, make sure you make a counteroffer quickly. This can help offset the anchoring impact of the other party's first offer. Be prepared. You don't want to improvise these parameters and numbers.

No unilateral concessions

This is perhaps the most common challenge to overcome. Know exactly what concessions you would be willing to offer in exchange for others. Have this in mind before the discussion and think beyond money. You could expand this to include other perks, aspects such as delivery time, provide access or information, resources, scope, expertise, support and so many other areas. Pick your battles. If you concede without getting anything, make sure it's an exception and not the norm. It's OK if it's a strategic move to generate higher or different results in the future.

Separate the issue from the people

Let's say you need to negotiate with someone whom you dislike, or know something about their persona of which you disapprove. How easy or hard would it be for you to negotiate with that individual? Here's the issue. The more you are able to separate that person from what you want from them in your mind, the better outcomes you'll get. Don't attack them, don't get angry; listen to them. Otherwise their defence mechanism will kick in, communication shuts down and the focus is no longer on your aim. Your tone – how you say it – if using a condescending tone, sarcasm or being passive-aggressive will backfire, even if the words are right.

Silence is king

In a negotiation, when someone drops an offer, what follows should be silence. If you make an offer and there's silence which makes you feel uncomfortable, you'll feel the need to make an immediate counteroffer. No, wait. You won't do this again, not after reading this book, my friend. You'll get comfortable with a few awkward seconds of silence. Usually what follows is a yes, a counteroffer or a question. Avoid negotiating with yourself. In this example, Dr Low had to work extra hard on this one, since silence in a conversation can be very culturally influenced. You want to use this strategy in a smart, adaptable way.

Bake a bigger cake

In a negotiation, many feel the cake is small and when one party gets something, the other loses. A collaborative outcome is when there are many options to grow the cake. Think of negotiating as a package, a bundle of options that belong together, instead of battling each issue. Always start from where there are commonalities and areas in which you both agree, and drive towards areas of disagreement. Trust me, you'll experience less resistance. For example, Dr Low suggested she could offer to mentor on Fridays, the day for which she was requesting flexible hours. Her senior managers were pleased to see that offer on the table. She leveraged this to request a more flexible schedule. She also applied the principle of getting everything in writing. A promise made in a negotiation when not written down can be a sailor's promise. It serves clarity and avoids conflict.

Be OK saying *'hasta la vista'* if necessary

Preparing to get a good deal is important, and preparing to walk away is too. Knowing when it's the right moment to walk away can be difficult. I get it, you don't want to end up in a bad situation/contract/conditions and at the same time you don't want to damage a professional relationship.

Walking away from a negotiation shouldn't be a bluffing strategy, instead an effective one. When you are not getting your BATNA at least, be OK to walk away. Not getting what you want now doesn't mean it won't ever happen. So a pertinent question is 'if not now, when?' Walk away gracefully, emotionally collected. Never burn a bridge. You never know when that person will cross your path in the future or when the chance will pop up again.

Dr Low played her cards well. She needed to be patient. In her part of the world, negotiations often take time and patience. Be aware of the negotiation practices in your culture. The basis applies, though the pace may vary.

What's the next negotiation you are getting ready for? Or the one you've been avoiding? With the right strategy, practice and timing, you'll increase your chances of getting what you need and want dramatically.

Key points Chapter 10

- As a smart woman in STEM like you, it's essential you know your worth and you ask for it.

- Let's disconnect the idea of having 'ambition' from selfishness and manipulation of others. Your ability to admit your ambition is related to whether or not you think you'll be able to achieve your goals and rewards.

- When it comes to salaries and financial remuneration at work, starting low has a lifelong impact.

- Whoever controls the start of a negotiation tends to control where it will end. So even if it's a bit scary, be the one to start the negotiation conversation.

- Pretty much every woman who I've coached in over 17 years (during training exercises and in real life situations) has first asked for too little (when she negotiates for herself and not for communal benefits). Few exceptions break this rule. So, trust me when I say, to the number you've got in mind to request, add at least 30-50% more. You'll be in the range of what other male peers will be aiming at.

- Get familiar with the '*if... then*' language. If I give you this, then I get that. That avoids giving in unilateral concessions. Practise this one before you need, since many women avoid this language out of obsolete socialisation patterns.

- As a smart woman in STEM know that separating the issue from the people is key. While you may like/dislike your professors, your boss or stakeholders, what you are negotiating about has little to do with the character of the people at the table, but a lot with what they are motivated about or their fears.

- Silence is your friend during a negotiation, so rehearse being comfortable with silence after you've made an offer. Don't negotiate with yourself.

- Use powerful negotiation skills to get work/lab space, to get published, to make more money, to close contracts, to leverage your network and get what you need to make a difference in the future.

11.
WOMEN SUPPORTING WOMEN, ASSERTIVENESS AND HARDCORE TACTICS

"Empowered women empower women."

ANONYMOUS AND TRUE

Take a look at these adjectives, and reflect on whether or not you could apply each of them to a woman at the same time:

- Powerful and also likeable

- Self-loving and caring for others

- Decisive and firm, yet flexible

- Communicative and expressive, yet a good listener

- Assertive and strong, and still approachable and friendly

To many people, these adjectives may sound contradictory and therefore negatively correlated, especially when describing women.

In this chapter, I want you to explore how you could consider two different worlds and make a convincing case: one world in which kindness, empathy and caring for others are core elements, and the other in which your wants, your needs and your decisiveness live. Why? When we are only displaying one part of these two worlds, either empathy − likeability − or strength and decisiveness, the opposite world is compromised.

I don't want to sugarcoat something that has been thoroughly researched by Harvard publications and the entire Lean In movement. The figures indicate that likeability and success are negatively correlated for women. The more powerful and strong a woman is, the less she is liked by both genders. Numbers have been crunched, especially in the tech industry and the world of politics. Unfortunately, though, we don't see much difference in STEM fields, where on top of their abilities and acceptance by others, women are also scrutinised on their IQ level.

Women often feel they walk the gender tightrope. A fragile state between being perceived as 'too masculine or too aggressive' and 'too feminine or too nice'. As a result, women are often at a disadvantage, some for being great at delivering outstanding business results, though on the downside being a little too aggressive, pushy and too focused on themselves. The flipside is that women are also disdained if they are too caring, warm and likeable. Women who are too accommodating and non-assertive don't get taken into consideration for leading the most exciting opportunities and challenging projects, because they don't show self-confidence.

Does that mean women are always disliked more than men when they reach a certain level of success? No, what research indicates is that women are more heavily penalised when they display behaviour in ways that violate gender stereotypes. And there are gender stereotypes and biases everywhere, even in some of the most advanced civilisations.

Due to socialisation patterns instilled at an early age, women are expected to be nice, caring, warm, friendly, not leaders, and somehow adopt nurturing roles in teams. The challenge may arise when a woman asserts herself or shows she's competitive. If she dares to make her team perform or be more competitive, if her behaviour is decisive, or if she displays a forceful or a thorough leadership style, then social expectations aren't fulfilled. Interestingly the same behaviours displayed by men in the workplace are often seen as expected traits of decisive leadership.

As a coach, I'm confronted with this topic because I'm often brought in to work on individual coaching sessions for senior leaders in global organisations. When HR calls me to work with a female executive on a one-to-one basis, the topic is mostly because she's been getting bad reviews from peers on being too aggressive or forceful in her decisions. These are women who, for the most part, generate outstanding business results. On the other hand, I often suggest HR teams identify senior male managers who get similar reviews so I can also get to work with them. The frequency of these cases is significantly less. So is it true that the majority of women at the top are aggressive? Of course not. Though when they 'violate' the beliefs about what women 'should' be like, they also generate pushback from others, being too masculine or too tough. Interestingly this feedback comes from both men and women.

Make no mistake, I do believe that whenever a leader, female or male, overuses power and uses force to manage others, that leadership is not effective, it damages teams, it leaves significant scars and it alienates talent. So there are both bad female and male leaders. No question about it. In fact, in a later chapter, we'll dive into how to deal with bad bosses and make your life easier. For now, I want you to explore why this phenomenon and disdain work, and what you can do to prevent it or stop its impact when you see it happen.

Girls and young women need role models

Having good role models in the early stages of life to inspire girls and young women to follow in areas that are not typically associated with women in the workplace is essential. In STEM fields and business, we know for a fact that by the age of 10-11 an interest in science has shown up in girls and statistically at the age of 15 it drops dramatically.

What can we do to stop this? Give visibility to super role models for women with a diverse background who are leaders in their areas. Let's make science and technology cool and accessible. Think about it. Who did you admire when you were growing up? In the world of science for example, we were surrounded by illustrations and male names as great scientists. But, I would have loved to have heard more about Ada Lovelace in the 19th century whose contribution is widely regarded as the first computer programmer. Or Rita Levi-Montalcini's grit and work in the field of neurological health in the brain (Nobel Prize winner in 1986) and currently Ginni Rometty, CEO of IBM and Meg Whitman, CEO of Hewlett Packard and her relentless efforts for diversity in the workplace. I'd like to see them featured more and more to inspire our girls and young women to go on, especially when it gets the message through.

Women supporting other women

I know that empowered women empower women. So where does this complexity come from when women need to support other women? Let's see. Can you recommend a film which I can show my nine-year-old niece in which she can see girls or women helping each other? And before you suggest sisters Elsa and Anna in *Frozen*, think again.

Women who help each other – not necessarily family – who, in fact, talk to each other and work together to achieve something more important than fighting for the affections of the prince in the film? Can you mention one film? Hard, right? Lately, we've seen a few examples since the entertainment industry was shown up by this raw reality, as there were no such role models for girls. For boys, there are plenty, from Batman and Robin to the current most popular computer games featuring male characters who fight and save the world together.

It's within our power to make sure we help girls and young women have those amazing stories and characters of badass women in STEM, and other fields that inspire them. They already exist and they are current, and yes, it's possible to be strong without having to lead or speak, walk or talk like a man, to lead effectively.

Women and power

Let's talk about power. You may or may not hold positional power. If your name is displayed at the highest levels of an organisation chart, you may enjoy hierarchical power.

Let's talk personal power. Personal power is the one you take with you all the time, regardless of your situation, the place you are at, regardless of your role or your salary. It's within you. It includes your ability and skill to influence people and events whether or not you have any formal authority.

When I first started coaching in 2002, I led an assertiveness course for corporate women. The groups were always oversubscribed. We described assertive and unassertive behaviour. Asserting yourself is not something only a few people get to do, it's something we all have the chance, and right, to do. Choosing our aims, attitudes and actions is an expression of personal power.

When you can choose your next action, regardless of another stimulus and you do it with positive energy, that is personal power. Being your own best self is real power, while you keep yourself accountable for emotions and impact. What would you use your power for? It can be your way to make progress, evolve and have your needs and wants met. It can accelerate the impact you want to have.

You don't have be a 'doormat' or the 'witch' at work

Let me explain, a human 'doormat' is someone who takes a passive approach to work and relationships, without standing up for themselves. They let others walk all over their wants and needs. The witch or *b. word*, on the other hand, is a complete opposite to that. Good news is you don't need to be any of those to get what you want. There's a 'sweet spot' that an assertive smart woman can find.

Among other things an assertive person can:

- Express positive feelings

- Express negative feelings

- Say no without letting guilt get in the way

- Give an honest opinion

- Qualify and express emotions clearly

- Set healthy boundaries

- Reach her ultimate goals while having high-quality human relationships

People pleasers don't get what they want

If you are non-assertive, at best you are passive and at worst a 'doormat' for others. You may find that others have no problem in stepping on your rights and ignoring your requests. You may be displaying one or more of these behaviours: no self-expression of your needs, feelings and own ideas to others, ignoring your rights and letting others step on them. What's the price you are paying for this?

If you enter the room in a shy or disempowering way, people will treat you with disrespect or pay little attention to you, instead of perceiving you as the valuable contributor which I know you really are. If this is you, you know you have to change. Your values, goals and dreams are too important to allow others to step on them. If you are backed into this particular corner, you are letting others decide for you, and make choices for you. It's worth noticing that passive behaviour is also unfair to others. Why? Because it can be interpreted as dishonest, indirect and misleading. Others will not necessarily notice how unhappy or frustrated you might be if you habitually accommodate them. Ultimately, this behaviour isn't positive or sustainable in the long run. It takes its toll on relationships and results, and eventually on your physical and emotional state.

If you know your boss or peers are simply taking advantage of you because you are being too accommodating, too nice, too compliant, you are also making it very convenient for them to mistreat you. You are probably interrupted, ignored in meetings, your ideas are not heard, or the most exciting projects are not falling on your desk. My guess is that if you are living in the passive corner, you are often working overtime, doing other people's jobs, helping out a little too much, and feeling guilty if you don't accommodate. Don't despair. You can regain power without ruining your relationships. Stick with me.

My way or the highway

On the other hand, if you are getting what you want, though at the expense of others or damaging relationships along the way, it's possible you are in the opposite corner, my friend. There are people who want to win, no matter what. In business and in life they get their way, they get what they want and often at the costs of other people's wants and needs. If they also do this in an aggressive way (verbal and non-verbal cues) then the consequences are often devastating, even if they get expected results. When that is the norm, and they make almost no exceptions, these people lose talent in their teams, demoralise peers and stakeholders. People who work for them, given the choice, would choose otherwise.

I've been coaching women on this particular topic for almost two decades. Here's what I've found. More often than not, a woman who displays aggressive behaviour in the workplace very likely used to be in 'doormat' mode, and one day, she decides 'no more'. An overcompensation of behaviour occurs and she ends up on the complete opposite side of the scale, using it as a self-defence mechanism.

Passive-aggressive toxic people

People who are passive-aggressive mask feelings like anger and frustration, and unfortunately project them on to others. Most passive-aggressive people are purposeful and intentional about their behaviours. They usually see a zero-sum game. Some symptoms of this are withdrawal, procrastination over important things, inefficient performance, hidden revenge attitudes, denial of anger, sarcasm, silent treatment, being critical, running late, amongst other traits. At its core, there is an underlying fear and avoidance of direct conflict, and also a sense of powerlessness and helplessness. You need to deal with them? Confront them directly face to face, rather than through an indirect form of communication such as email or telephone. Stay calm during your conversation, and ask open-ended questions to ascertain the reasons behind the person's behaviour and set clear standards and boundaries. There's a good chance you'll find a way to work together after this.

The art of saying "no"

In order to say no to something or someone, there's no need to lie, to over explain ourselves or make excuses. Declining is enough. Easier said than done, right? This is one of the most common issues I coach women about. I can relate to this from my experiences in my earlier IT years. Finding the sweet spot of assertiveness as part of your updated version of yourself also means you'll say no to people and projects that no longer serve the purpose and intention you've set for yourself and your career. If you have been too accommodating, you may find this step really hard. At first you won't be completely guilt-free and over time you'll start harvesting the benefits of regaining your power, your energy and your time. You'll see, it gets easier.

A few pointers: do say the word no, and if you feel like adding gratitude it won't hurt – no, thanks. Be short, don't go on. Trust your gut, when the answer makes you shrink and feel anxious, it's very likely you need to say no. If instead the answer to the question makes you expand (literally) then you know your answer, too. If needed, you may use the word 'because' and keep it short, or provide another alternative if you want. Don't use an apologetic tone of voice. Finally, decrease or eliminate rumination afterwards. It's a waste of energy. Simplify your life and propel your career by learning to say no.

Double jeopardy?

Women often have to provide more evidence of competence than men in order to be seen as equally proficient. This phenomenon is often referred as the 'Prove-It-Again' challenge. Recent studies indicate that women in STEM face more challenges in their field to prove their value. Prove-It-Again bias, at the core, is the perceived mismatch between the typical woman and the typical brilliant scientist. Women's mistakes tend to be noticed more and remembered longer, while their success is often attributed to luck, and men's success stories are attributed to skill.

Be assertive in the way you highlight your worth, get clear about the value you add, and be resilient in the process. It's all part of being assertive, in spite of this phenomenon.

Spot your biggest challenges and overcome them

You know when someone 'pushes your buttons'. Well, most people have buttons which trigger specific reactions or responses. When I talk about assertiveness it works the same way. You need to know them well and control them before they control you.

Some people tend to adopt a 'doormat' mode in front of authority figures and then find their assertive sweet spot in front of their peers. The problem is that those changes of attitude leave people knowing you can be unpredictable or unreliable. Some other people are assertive at work and a total 'doormat' at home or in front of strangers.

Take Giulia, a C-suite manager in a food engineering company. She had made significant progress as a team leader and a communicator. Or at least I thought so, until I had the chance to see her in action at a steering committee event. She was coming across as an accommodating people pleaser, instead of the power player she was. Fortunately, she was open to feedback and I raised awareness about this aspect. For most of us, the assertive/passive/aggressive mode stories start in our early stages of childhood or early work life. So our adult badass version needs an upgrade. Regardless of what your natural reaction or trigger has been until now, it's time to review how and what you can do to find your sweet spot, the right assertive zone, more often and with less trouble.

Context and culture matter

What is too direct in one setting is soft in another. Be smart about when and how you adapt this behaviour. Sometimes you'll need to adjust your style to the receiver. The organisational culture will also help you find out what you need to adjust to find your sweet spot.

You want to be very smart in the way you adapt your style and assertive behaviour using the spectrum of possibilities. If you are in an organisation or a country or culture where you'd describe assertive and decisive behaviour as expected and acceptable, you'll be able to express it accordingly.

You are looking for the signals that indicate you are in such an organisation when:

- People place value on direct communication (oral and written)

- Players attempt to have control or regulate the environment

- People value competition, success and advancement

- Strong players are praised or admired

- Trust is based on people's capabilities and often results are valued over people

So, if those things describe the place you work in, you can use and adapt your communication style to meet the environment by using the higher spectrum of the assertive scale and still be perceived as a positive player and team member.

On the other hand, perhaps your organisation or environment has the following traits:

- People value cooperation, warm relationships and make sure that 'nobody loses face'

- Teams value harmony and often communicate more indirectly, expressing the importance of values, tradition or experience

- They see others as trustworthy people because they are part of the organisation

- People have a high sense of equality, solidarity and quality of life and not so much of competition

When you decide to adapt the way you express assertiveness, you are not being unauthentic, you're being smart.

You may be in organisations with a particular hybrid style which has a bit of both. Be wise, know who is involved in the dynamics of the situation(s) you wish to change and regain more assertiveness finding the sweet spot. Then adjust your compass accordingly.

The magic of this is that you can wisely adapt your style without sacrificing your wants and needs. Trust me it's possible.

How to be assertive without getting the B* title

OK, even if you're smart, collected and tough, standing up for yourself can be hard sometimes. Regardless of where in the world, I've seen in all five continents, women aren't supposed to rock the boat, they are expected to care and defuse conflict, accommodate and not challenge the status quo. Therefore, asking for anything that doesn't comply with those expectations can seem transgressive or even make you earn the B* title at work. Here's how to get over that, and get what you want.

Step by step. This is the assertiveness model or sweet spot model I use to coach women.

It can serve you too.

1. Identify your buttons. Specifically ask yourself if your triggers are people close to you, strangers, people in authority, different cultures or groups, or if it has to do with handling pressure. List them, have them on the radar and be especially aware when they pop up.

2. Be aware of your natural mode (passive – aggressive – passive/aggressive or mostly assertive).

3. Pick low-stress situations to play with. Select one or two scenarios which you want to start working on, where the stakes are not high and you are prepared to allow yourself to rehearse these first steps.

4. Start by adapting your verbal and non-verbal communication. One change at a time. You want to display firm and non-apologetic behaviour that is human and respectful. A combination of a firm presence with the ability to connect with others.

a. Use statements that suggest a compromise or collaboration

b. Ask for a time-out when needed

c. Ask for clarification instead of 'assuming'

d. Use 'I' statements

e. Use verbs that show more responsibility and action; be emphatic when you communicate

f. Avoid sugarcoating your message, so it's not confusing; achieve this by using verbs like *will* instead of could or should, *want* instead of need, or *choose to* instead of have to

5. Make your request. This step, for many women, is the tough one. It's about voicing what you want, even if you have never requested it before or have waited for a long time. This is the moment you are aiming at getting what you need or to set a boundary. You want to do this in a clear and confident way. Be a good listener and yet, if you face resistance, it's time to reframe your argument and ask again. Don't be discouraged by objections or questions. Even if the answer is no, don't leave the conversation without suggesting a timeframe to revise it or follow up again.

6. Breathe. If you are sensitive to time and impatient (similarly, sometimes I know I am), breathe. Take your time. If drama erupts on the other side of the table, resist the temptation to pull out your sword and fight. Stay calm and collected whenever possible.

7. You can't change people. You can only fully take responsibility for your own words and actions. Being respectful and clear is your best way to continue expressing your wants and needs.

8. If you get what you want, bravo, *chica*! If you don't, avoid falling into the trap of rumination – the bad habit of repetitively going over a thought or a problem without conclusion. If you let it rest on your shoulders, it can lead to depression or anxiety. So don't.

In which area of your life or career are you required to show more assertiveness and find the sweet spot between your wants/needs and those of others? When you tackle this one, you'll discover you can be both strong and firm at the same time, and also empathetic and caring. It's time to recognise that as women, we can be grateful for what we have and at the same time ask for what we need.

Key points Chapter 11

- You can be strong and caring. You can be competent, confident and decisive while you are also humane, friendly and a smart woman in STEM. You don't have to trade one for the other.

- In old leadership paradigms, people would label soft skills as feminine traits: empathy, vulnerability, humility, generosity, patience, etc). The same obsolete views of male traits in leaders have been: task-focused, strong, ego-driven, powerful, assertive, competitive, stubborn or direct. It's time to re-write these rules and expectations. Women and men can add value by having a good mix of those sets of skills. We need good leaders regardless of their gender, leaders who are future-ready. In the 4th Industrial Revolution, if we are to thrive together we need to value such skills as human skills and not gender-specific skills.

- The numbers don't lie. Most at the top of STEM fields are men. If the scarcity of power has originated this effect it isn't really our fault though it's our problem. We need more examples and role models to show how women can support each other. Let's upgrade ourselves so we women can also succeed in the new era.

- It's time women actively support and endorse each other. It's time we verbally sponsor and uplift other women in the workplace – in your next meeting, conference call or email. Now. Today.

- The success of every woman should be inspiration and fuel to another.

12.
BAD BOSSES, QUEEN BEES AND GREAT BOSSES

"Don't let anyone rob you of your imagination, your creativity, or your curiosity. It's your place in the world; it's your life. Go on and do all you can with it, and make it the life you want to live."

MAE JEMISON, FIRST AFRICAN-AMERICAN WOMAN ASTRONAUT
IN SPACE, NASA

OK, I already mentioned that between a stimulus and your reaction or response, there's a window of opportunity to decide how you proceed. You'll create an impact on your outcomes accordingly. Sometimes you'll get what you want, sometimes you won't; you'll survive and move on.

Difficult bosses may challenge us and we'll need to choose between reacting and responding. They at times defy logic. Some blissfully ignore the negative impact that they have on their teams. Others seem to even get satisfaction from the toxicity or chaos they create around them. Either way, they tend to generate stress in others.

The smart ninja set

Remember those amazing ninja characters in films? After this chapter you'll be able to manage your boss like one. An office ninja knows how to be strong but stay calm, is prepared, agile, disciplined and very smart. When your boss pushes your buttons, you'll require an extra set of abilities, the ninja set for you, smart woman in STEM.

When you develop the ability to remain calm and manage your emotions around them, this will have an impact on your performance and wellbeing. The chance is high you'll never know the origin of their story, what shaped them and why they are so hard to interact with. So this chapter will provide a few practical tools and a new approach. Discover how to deal with, cope with and even thrive when you have a terrible boss. Bad bosses come in all genders. You'll also discover how to spot great bosses and learn from them. Remember, you are in control of far more than you realise.

Now, I'm typing this chapter while I am working with leaders in one of the kindest places on earth, the Kingdom of Bhutan. This tour also took me to Bangkok, Thailand where I worked with leaders in tech. It's been an inspiring and exciting experience, because one common factor in this region is that kindness is regarded as one of the essential virtues we can have and experience. Being kind to yourself is something to remember when you learn to deal with difficult people. Making your work and your wellbeing one of your top priorities is key. It's a sign of self-respect and self-care. After all, you can't stop the waves, but you can learn how to surf.

My worst boss crossed my path when I was in technology. A popular bully. He was popular in high power circles, yet he was a bully and a jerk to his subordinates. He held low ethical standards, and I knew I couldn't work for him and his team, who would follow suit. That made it easy for me to decide to look for another job and leave. He taught me how I never wanted to lead a team. Thanks to him I saw lousy leadership first-hand. I was able to spot good leaders quickly after that. I discovered I had to learn the rule book, I also learned to recognise that some rules can be broken or reshaped. I learned about good governance and these lessons remained with me decades after that bad experience.

One thing is for sure, people remember the worst and the best of all kinds. The ones in the middle are easy to forget. You remember them because of the way they made you feel. Safe or at risk. Listened to or ignored. Respected or humiliated. Significant or ghost-like.

Think of your absolute best teacher or mentor at school or in your career. How did she/he make you feel? What did you learn about yourself in that process?

As it is today, and as shown by the Employee Engagement Survey by Gallup, around 50% of employees who have left jobs did so due to bad managers at some point.

To be fair, there are reasons why some people get to be evil bosses; even good guys get to be bad bosses. They either lacked proper training or it's their first time managing people. Or maybe they lacked good role models. If all you see are bad examples of something, you may get to imitate them in an attempt to do what you feel is expected of you. Sometimes it's the system; look, if you and your boss are in a system that only praises task performance and cost reduction, and there's no time to invest in other areas of leadership or development, it's not surprising that's all they do. The old school of carrots and sticks has left scars in bad management systems. Unfortunately, it's still alive in academia, in science, and in many areas of engineering. This approach, in fact, reduces productivity and it can be disempowering.

Are STEM fields more fertile soil for bad bosses than other areas? The apparent imbalance of representation of power in male-dominated STEM fields sometimes makes the relationship between stakeholders in powerful positions and the rest a perfect setting for bullying to take place in. Since career advancement is at stake, it makes it hard for people in low or middle ranks to report it. If a player advances because she/he is seen as an expert in a field, it doesn't necessarily mean she/he has the appropriate people skills to lead a team. They can be great as scientists or engineers and it would probably be best for many of them to remain so. Most of these become bosses because of time or experience. If this was your boss's path, and she/he developed a bully personality, it ends up being a professional jeopardy for the trainees and employees. In many cases, in science fields for example, there's often no clear HR role or advisor for HR matters who may offer guidance.

I've come across too many of my coachees who put up with a bad boss for way too long because the idea of a dream job inspires them, or because they love what they get to do. However, bad bosses who create stress on others take a toll on mental, emotional and even physical health. Surprisingly, some employees who are abused still doubt whether or not their experience qualifies as bullying or mobbing at work, and they try to ignore or overlook negative signs.

Have you ever experienced any of these situations?

- Your boss establishes impossible deadlines that will set you up to fail

- Your superior withholds necessary information or even goes as far as giving you wrong information on purpose

- Obvious offensive oral or written jokes and derogative/humiliating comments

- She/he spreads malicious rumours and untrue information, gossips behind your back

- Your boss tries to isolate you in social settings and intimidates you whenever possible

- Your boss is the bottleneck preventing you from achieving your job/a deserved promotion

- She/he harasses you physically or verbally

- You find your boss intrudes into your private life, no boundaries are respected

- Explosive, yelling, loss of temper and acting unprofessionally against you

- Being two-faced, one treating you like a jerk when you two are alone and another being the nice guy when in public

- Preventing you from advancing your career, sabotaging training or mentorship opportunities for you

And the list goes on.

If you can answer yes to any of these questions, your boss, and therefore your work environment, is toxic.

Today bullying is complex in our organisations. It is unacceptable for everyone, though research shows that it can take an even higher toll on employees or trainees who have a foreign background. Why? They are mainly vulnerable as targets due to the social isolation that can occur when a person is new to a country, city or working place.

Monk, a Singaporean mathematician working for a risk insurance company, came seeking advice while feeling entirely bullied by her alpha-male boss. She was alone in a German-speaking city. We worked on a few strategies that could help her regain her self-confidence. She needed to establish healthy boundaries and find her tribe and 'allies' at work so she could get stronger. It took her at least another six months to feel she could decide to stay and further her career.

Let me suggest you be bold and smart about this. You may decide you want to leave. In which case, I advise you to design a strategic path to follow. Should you decide to stay and don't give up that job or dream, this section includes a few bad boss typologies and strategies I'd like you to have at your disposal. *Your personal Swiss Army knife* against bosses from hell, if you will. First, you'll have to identify your bad boss's typology and then get to work, like a smart ninja.

Narcissistic know-it-all

This boss from hell displays an obnoxious level of self-esteem. A conceited, egoistical person who loves to put people down. His/her favourite subject is 'me, myself and I'. She/he can be tricky at first because she/he can usually sell and pitch an idea to people who don't know them, especially people in power or new stakeholders.

Your best weapon: a response; your worst tactic: a reaction and allowing your boss's attacks to get under your skin. Do not, and I repeat, do not, feed the beast. Don't foster this lousy behaviour or give it too much attention. They can only survive because there are enablers to help them perpetuate their attacks and people who decide to turn a blind eye to them and keep silent.

Be collected, cool and disengaged whenever possible. Deep breathing, a few yoga lessons can help you keep cool under stress. Keep an eye on the ball, remind yourself why you are there in the first place. Keep a record of incidents and events; you may need it at some point to do some fact checking. When upset, take a step back, regain energy and reconnect. When addressing him/her, focus exclusively on facts and information, not on the emotional charge or remarks.

The people pleaser

Your boss is lacking decisiveness and is a people pleaser. Your boss avoids conflict, especially with authority, and doesn't want to exert power. This affects you of course, since she/he is unable to set boundaries around workload and is unassertive. This type of boss will leave the team in a somewhat harmonious state, though unsure if the work is done and where the project is going. With this type of persona as a boss, it's likely that the most challenging, exciting projects might not fall on your boss's desk. The organisation's results may suffer.

You should take this aspect into account when drawing your career strategy because you won't see the benefits of good leadership in this position. Take Lucía, a senior program manager in a technology company. She was able to spot her boss's need to please superiors and the head of the department at every significant milestone. It often resulted in long weekends of overload for the team, and in the long run, the cool projects were assigned to a parallel group. After attending an empowering session with myself and one of my partners, she knew she needed to plan her mid-term strategy and move to another area. She couldn't see herself growing under that position. She's now thriving at a higher level in the same organisation.

The control freak

This boss's micromanagement style kills creativity and innovation. The root of their problem, like many others, is in their past. Your boss's micromanaging style is not something you can change, though you can learn how to provide reassurance and gain trust, little by little. Many of them are excellent solo players and it becomes an issue when they are assigned as team leaders. They are unable to lead, to get everyone on board, to delegate and empower others. They distrust pretty much everyone, and because innovation and failure go hand in hand, and are essential in STEM fields, this is a problem. Be proactive, let him/her know you are on top of things, avoid confrontation, it's pointless. Do this enough times and she/he will increase trust and release some pressure. One of his/her biggest fears is to be taken advantage of, so make sure you provide reassurance when you communicate.

Several years ago, I started working as an external executive coach in the German part of Switzerland. My main stakeholder in HR is in this category. She would say things like: "Gabriela, I want you to be creative and innovative in your programmes, but check with me first every time." I quickly recognised she felt insecure in her role, and it extended to her team and even external players like myself. Knowing that micromanagers want to feel in control, I started proactively providing updates every Monday morning, before she even had time to request them. I also made sure milestones were noted and kept thorough records. Our relationship improved over time. We still work together, and I notice she's much more relaxed when she deals with me. We have developed more trust over time. She still micromanages other employees and providers though, just not me anymore.

The ghost

If you rarely see your boss in the office or lab and get little response via email or no face time at all, oh well, dear, your boss in this category. She/he may say how much employee engagement is critical or even how much they care, though they are absent, due to work or personal stuff. You are not given feedback and/or guidance. My first suggestion is, don't fall into the trap of feeling demotivated or lost. It's not about you. Keep making sure your performance is outstanding and noticed by other stakeholders who are present. If possible, spot how/who can give you the necessary go-ahead to get your job done when she/he isn't around. Depending on your seniority or experience, this boss isn't so bad if you are looking for autonomy and room to experiment and create. On the other hand, if you feel you need or want more guidance, this is an opportunity for you to get to establish relationships with other key people and stakeholders. Be sure to contribute and show results; more often than not, people will be willing to support a resourceful, smart woman like you.

The fifty shades at work

A flirtatious boss isn't really what you want as a mentor, leader or role model. Though we still see this type of boss around and especially in areas where power is unevenly distributed. There's no question that the most recent global #MeToo movement has brought light to many workplaces that still foster misogyny and harassment.

Unfortunately, in STEM areas this phenomenon also finds fertile soil in which to flourish. Often location plays a role. A few examples are research labs, or remote locations used for research purposes with male teams, and quiet isolated stations for research; or fields where a woman is overseen by a tenured male adviser who holds superpowers over a person's future career. Those are all factors that can potentially foster these situations. Over the past few years, more high-profile cases have come to light and women have broken the silence. The winds of change are here. Should you find yourself in one of these unfortunate situations, here's what I want you to know. First, it's not about you. This situation often takes a horrible toll on a woman's sense of worth and self-esteem. Silence and secrecy can only make it worse.

I recommend using three levels of tactics. The first is often enough, and it's based on you not even acknowledging the unpleasant compliment or teasing comment. Keep talking as if you haven't understood it and keep being professional. You signal no interest at all. Should the flirtatious advancement go on, you can now be more direct. Once you are sure inappropriate behaviour is going on, it's time to address it directly. Showing shyness at this point can be counterproductive and things can escalate quickly. Be concrete and firm. Watch out for your body language around him; you want to avoid sending a message that may be misleading or mismatching your firm request for the behaviour to stop. Finally, be aware of the sexual harassment policy in your institution, be sure to know the channels and format for complaints if necessary. And remember, this type of harassment is violating human rights beyond your organisation's policies.

Make sure you are not alone, seek emotional support and legal advice, and don't let this take a toll on your self-esteem. Know you are there on your merits and not because someone decided to give you a position based on your looks, gender or any other aspect.

Real Queen Bee

A Queen Bee is often associated with the old and now more outdated stereotype of a woman who mistreats her subordinates and has sacrificed everything to get high up in the ranks.

I can explain the next strategies on how to deal with tough bosses and how to thrive, though I thought it was important not to rush to label your female boss as a Queen Bee simply because she shows strength and assertiveness. The real Queen Bee is a dictatorial and aggressive boss whose male counterpart can be called the King Wasp, showing the same behaviours. We simply tend to evaluate them differently. It's a stereotype I'd like to encourage you to examine and rethink if you catch yourself using it.

She expects everyone else to do the same. She shows no sympathy for other women and their responsibilities, linked to different roles (like motherhood). Here it's fair to say that women face a double bind. It's a predicament many women in leadership face: women are 'damned if they do, doomed if they don't'. If they display a somewhat tough style, to be a hardliner with a firm view, they are perceived as too masculine. They are labelled too quickly as Queen Bees. If they are too soft, they are seen as less decisive and lacking in confidence. In other words, men are often expected to take charge and women are supposed to nurture and care for the collective good of all. Interestingly, even though many women I've coached who think other women make good managers, when asked to choose, they would choose a man to report to as their boss. How about you? Given a choice, would you choose to report to a man or a woman?

Now, if in all honesty your boss is a real Queen Bee, or its male version the King Wasp for that matter, and the persuasion strategies don't work, make sure you don't fall into the trap. Resist the temptation to respond in kind. Even if it seems tempting, juicy and rewarding, it's a short-term tactic. Another thing you want to avoid is venting in your own workplace about her, as this can backlash faster than a fighter jet. Do keep a record of your results (especially feedback from other stakeholders or clients), as this may come in handy if you need to defend your performance against subjective views.

You want to make sure there are clear and objective criteria to measure your target and performance. If there's no system, keep records, measure your performance and keep track over time. Avoid having spontaneous essential conversations with this type of boss, instead be ready. Make sure you set up time and space to talk to her. Keep your records at hand and address factual information, avoid emotionally charged expressions.

Make sure that you still remain open to any important and useful pieces of feedback that your difficult female boss may have for you. I often see women completely disregarding feedback from bosses they can't stand, simply because of their personality or a difficult relationship. Make sure you don't miss critical feedback because of this.

As an ultimate resource, before considering leaving to move to another department, you can explore having another party or HR staff present in an appraisal conversation. This is a hard path to take, though one that can set a limit and set the record straight.

Why it is crucial to kill the Queen Bee syndrome to thrive in the 4th Industrial Revolution

The scarcity of power has been planted among us as women, or perceived as such by many. Scarcity since we often see only one woman sitting at the highest level of the decision-making table. Even though we didn't start this issue, it's our problem to solve.

If we are to thrive in this new era, we need to start supporting each other and cheering each other on. Let's be the role models that Millennials see and Generation Z will learn that women do support each other.

Remember, just like difficult people, Queen Bees don't just happen. They've usually got baggage and a story behind them. You may never get to figure them out or know why they feel compelled to make other women's lives hard, though one thing is for sure, there's a reason for their behaviour.

I was invited to help a team define a long-term brand strategy in the French part of Switzerland. I was cautiously warned that Suzanne, the 'time bomb' would be there. She had been promoted to a senior position after several years and now she had to supervise her former peers. She was described to me as a royal Queen Bee: intolerant, a poor listener, impatient, thin-skinned and insecure. To my enormous surprise, when Suzanne entered the room it was the very same Suzanne – energetic businesswoman I had met a decade ago at an event in London. We stayed in touch for a few years because of common coaching interests. Her husband got a significant physical disability, and she unexpectedly became the primary breadwinner and caregiver for her husband and child back in those days. A few more grey hairs, but she greeted me with a bright smile. After recalling a few good memories, she went on to tell me she was having a tough time leading this particular team. She had applied for another senior position and was given this one. Her family situation had worsened since London and she was about to reach burn-out. She was glad I could help her define a strategy for her team. There are always two sides to every story, aren't there?

We certainly worked on defining the strategy, though we also tackled other issues that would allow her to get energised and focused as a newly appointed leader. This helped her declutter bad communication patterns in the team, and over time, she was able to lead better and her team was able to get to a performing stage feeling safe.

Coming together in the 4th Industrial Revolution – call for action

Here's the thing. The way we women accelerate and increase our influence in the world is by supporting each other and helping each other thrive. No one else is going to do it for us. Either we create synergy amongst us, or we will miss out on valuable opportunities to make a difference in the world as an essential force representing 50% of its chance to improve and overcome global challenges.

A call for action for every smart woman reading this

In a male-dominated environment that surrounds several of those workplaces in which STEM women can add value, it's important for us to find support and offer support when it's possible.

The few women who are in the industry do need to stick together. It's necessary to find and be allies with each other. Don't forget that not all men are aware of this phenomenon and many of them want to be part of the solution, they just don't know how. Bring them on your side, many can champion and support women in this process.

What you can gain if there are more women in leadership roles

More women in the higher ranks help to narrow other gaps (including benefits from diversity and decreasing pay gaps). This can cause a chain reaction or ripple effect of benefits for women in the lower ranks. It translates into more possibilities to have additional female mentors, advocates, allies and female role models available.

More women ascending to higher ranks also means an end to the 'tokenism' we see in the workplace – this is when many women compete for the few spots available to them. Whereas in reality, all open seats should be available for both men and women.

Better business results generate better conditions for everyone. We settled this one before, we know organisations that have more female decision-makers get better financial performance, and in STEM areas, better organisations reach better KPIs (key performance indicators). That also means higher gains for everyone in the mid and long term.

If you are a woman in power

There are very concrete things you can do to thrive and create a stronger presence of women in your field.

Send the elevator down

Yes, if you are up there already or have a position of influence, being the first or only one doesn't mean a lot if you don't bring along the second and third woman to your team. You can do this by being smart and strategic. It will make your life easier, and you will be able to let your influence be heard and seen. Embrace your power and do not be afraid to risk your status.

Let your authentic female power shine

I know too many women who try to 'hide' the fact that they are women. Overcompensating and hiding feminine traits and replacing them with masculine traits is counterproductive. If you find yourself feeling like you need to emulate men to fit the existing power paradigm, you can stop and shift gears. Resist the inner critic voice telling you that you need to 'fit in' in that limiting way. Instead, trust yourself, be open to new ways of thinking and innovations that break the mould. Be you, be bold. Embrace who you are.

Share your story

Be aware of the fact that you are already influencing other women, and also men, in your career and your world. Share how you have achieved your success and overcome setbacks. Even if you think your story is not that special or unique, it is. It's yours. Younger women are looking for inspiration from people they see and observe and learn from their stories.

Make failure your fuel

This is a lesson coined more recently by Abby Wambach, the greatest soccer player of all times, in an epic speech to women. She suggests that, just as athletes do, we need to understand the gift of failure as fuel, and fuel is power. Should you have had bad experiences in your career that left scars, and failed, use this as your fuel to propel you to your next level. Upgrade yourself by starting again with a clean slate. This step is crucial if you are to succeed. So next time you see someone or something that reminds you of past unresolved issues, you will finally respond and not react to it. Include other women in your career. Don't assume stories are true or use unconscious bias to make decisions. When you see another woman succeed, cheer for her. Let's not hold different bars to attain recognition for other women compared to the ones you may hold for men in your career.

Endorse other women

Yes, genuinely praise another woman in front of others. Highlighting another woman's accomplishments in a given conversation, for example, while networking or during a meeting, can go a long way. Endorse other women by offering a direct recommendation, praise, an introduction to someone they can get to meet and benefit from, contribute by granting access to information or another contact. In other words, open the door for another woman. It's not that hard, it sounds simple, but it isn't the norm. We help others thrive, and we send a clear message: women support each other. We are allies and not competitors amongst ourselves.

Call crap and bad practices when you see them

When you see and hear crap or unconscious bias applied to women, don't be a bystander. It's time to speak up and to do it smartly, without aggressively waving the 'feminine flag'. It will kill your message. You can do this firmly and in a way that does not create backlash. Training or educating your male colleagues about gender intelligence is one of the smartest things senior female leaders can do. When you see different or unfair standards applied to the evaluation of women and men in publications, in hiring processes, work assignments, compensation schemes and promotions, it's time to speak up.

Change is here

Once I witnessed a senior C-suite power player, she was making her point when the board was selecting another senior leader. One of her colleagues said: "We can dismiss these CVs, they're women and we already have one on the board." She said with a kind smile: "OK Richard, then we can also skip those CVs, they are tall, white men. We already have some like these on the board." She suggested reviewing other, more important criteria to select the next player, such as negotiation skills, credentials and potential for growth. She continues to grow a fruitful relationship with her board, though she calls the truth when she sees it. She recently called me in to provide an effective unconscious bias programme to her board. They are realigning their hiring process as a result.

Being the solitary woman in a team, at C-Suite level or in a leadership role in a male-dominated environment can be isolating, and it hinders the chance you may have of moving things forward. To reach a critical mass of women in STEM and business as decision-makers, women must play an active role. We need to support each other and overcome the old reputation and the outdated idea that women can't work together or support other women. The time is now. We must play an active role. Change is here.

Spot a great boss so you can become one

Whether it's in tech companies, universities or boardrooms, I see that great bosses are hard to find, hard to leave and impossible to forget.

A good boss today is no longer limited by the traditional role of boss with a top-bottom approach. The current role of the new good boss is rather seen as 'gardener'. Yes, a *gardener* that makes people in their team grow and blossom as professionals and also as human beings. They have a team that performs better, are retained better and definitely made up of happier individuals.

I recall my best bosses. I often ask international audience members to describe their best boss. They usually skip innate traits such as looks, intelligence, or even academic credentials. Most people describe higher qualities: energy, empathy, passion, capacity to listen, integrity, respect, honesty or even their ability to assess risks.

A great boss connects a team's daily work with great goals and empowers them to achieve great things. She earns respect as a leader, not only obedience as a manager. She's thrilled to see her team achieve relevant milestones, and doesn't feel threatened by them. A good boss is able to see her people as people, with their stories and talents, and sees beyond weaknesses or gaps.

There are five things that I consistently see great bosses do:

Great bosses are like great chess players. They know each person on their team and recognise their unique abilities, strengths, weaknesses, what they appreciate and what they dislike. The result is a blend of teamwork orchestrated by a good boss with a strategic mind, knowing that his/her people are in fact, people.

Great bosses stand in front of the bus for their team. When danger comes, they pull their people from the risky spot whenever possible and remove obstacles. Opposite to bad bosses, who would throw their team under the bus to save face. When necessary, a good boss will clean up his/her team's mess, take responsibility for mistakes. If they can't stop the running bus, they'll stand in front of it and take the hit themselves. That's why the responsibility of leading a team is not for everyone. It requires sacrifice and courage.

Great bosses make you feel uncomfortable. Yes, in a way that inspires you to take risks, to grow and expand possibilities. They ask the same questions and milestones from you and any other male colleague to challenge status quo and expect the best of you. Even when you doubt yourself.

Great bosses are not afraid of giving critical feedback to their teams. They don't put off giving constructive criticism. They give it in the moment or on the very next chance they have to do it. They offer praise in public and critique in private. They know that even more important than feedback is to give constructive praise. They provide it a specific way, so instead of saying 'well done' they may be specific: *'This week's meeting I noticed how you were willing to question our CFO's vision on how challenging the projections for Q2 are. I really appreciate your confidence.'* In other words, they are proactive and specific.

Great bosses recognise they are only human and have their emotions in check. A person who's aware of his/her emotional state and knows his/her emotions well can manage stress and stressful situations with emotional intelligence. They don't shy away from expressing their own emotions in the right manner. They talk to their people as a person first, and then as their boss. They share information and knowledge in a generous way and avoid being secretive or making false promises.

Passionate and committed great bosses also help us shape who we become. Humble bosses who share credit and recognise and appreciate their people are wanted. Be the boss you'd like to have.

Key points Chapter 12

- Difficult bosses may challenge you and tend to generate stress in you and others.

- As a smart woman in STEM, you'll need from time to time a smart ninja set. This special toolbox will be useful to manage a bad boss and still get what you want and need.

- Bad bosses come in different flavours and in all genders. You are now better equipped to deal with a narcissistic know-it-all, with people pleasers, control freaks, flirty bosses and Queen Bees. Yes, we still have all those and more in the workplace. Your job is to know that you and your contribution are important. Trust yourself, your intuition and take action.

- This chapter explored the effective strategies you can put in place to be assertive and get what you want without hurting relationships. You don't have to get the Queen Bee title to get things done, or to play the 'office doormat' who's ignored, in order to try to be liked or accepted. You know there's a sweet spot. One where you can be a powerful woman who embraces her leadership in all its greatness, respecting others and achieving outstanding results.

- You can be assertive, achieve your goals and maintain long-lasting relationships.

13.
LIFE HACKS FOR WORKING STEM MUMS - ROCKSTARS!

"I always did something I was a little not ready to do. I think that's how you grow. When there's that moment of 'Wow, I'm not really sure I can do this' and you push through those moments, that's when you have a breakthrough."

MARISSA MAYER, CEO YAHOO

The top two questions that any working mum is asked: "How do you do it?" and "So you think it's possible to have it all?" I have yet to meet a working mum who hasn't had to answer one of those two 'mum-questions'.

Though in this episode, since I'm a mother of two super cool teenagers myself, I admit that whenever I have a chance to talk to female world leaders who are also mothers, I'm interested in knowing what their 'mum-hacks' are. The term 'working mother' is redundant, and I want to help women get better results with less trouble. For me STEM mums are simply rockstars.

I believe you can have it all, but very likely not at the same time. If you love what you do and the choices you make, that vision can drive you forward even during intense motherhood phases.

Just like STEM fields, motherhood is not for everyone, just like leadership, bungee-jumping or spicy food, having kids may not be your thing, and that's OK. If you have kids or are thinking about how to juggle the essential balls in life with kids, family, health or job, these hacks can help you.

I mentioned I come from a family where strong, caring women supported each other. I've been working since the age of 15. First giving out flyers on the streets in Mexico City to make some money over the holidays for school supplies, later serving tables at my internet café, then IT consulting, corporate training, and now coaching world leaders. It took some time, though I found the sweet spot in my career. I want you to reflect on this too, as you are making career-motherhood decisions. A sweet spot (Japanese call this *ikigai*, pronounced eye-ka-guy) is where you find your core talents and passions come together, to cover a need or solve a problem in the world and ideally the world is willing to pay for. I found my *ikigai* and how it serves the world. In your case, this need/problem is within science, tech, engineering or math to make this a better world. The drive to serve and continue to do so during and after motherhood happened in my life, and having clarity at the core of my *ikigai* is valuable. Under our website www.gabrielamueller.com/tools, you'll find the visual tool for your personal use.

Personally, I believe that a stay-home mum's job is also great and it's also one of the most demanding jobs there is. Being a mum or dad 24/7 at home has its complexity because everything spins around the kids' needs and there's no 'me-time'. The home making plus the children's pace can be super demanding. That said, I sincerely respect the decisions of women who decide to do it.

Now, to working mum hacks, a combination of strategies, based on my own experience and also advice from some of the top mothers in STEM. Interested? Stay with me.

ISSP is an international consortium of organisations that tackles essential subjects through social science research. Over the course of a decade, they surveyed and studied responses in regard to the effects of work and motherhood. Their 'Family and Changing Gender Roles' study found the following among the key findings.

Good for the kids

Women who were brought up by mothers who had a job outside the home are more likely to hold leadership or management positions, are more likely to achieve supervisory roles in those jobs, and also to earn higher incomes for the family than those who were brought up by mothers who stayed at home on a full-time basis. Interestingly, men brought up by working mothers are more likely to take care of household chores and also spend more time taking care of the family.

Better finances

More resources and advantages are provided for the family. Over time, women who return to being financially active in life are in a better state to secure future savings, investments and retirement plans than those who don't.

Happy mum – happy child

If you are a working mum and pursue your wants, and you acknowledge your values and needs, you will find this a fulfilling journey to continue along. I did not say it will be a smooth ride, though it will be fulfilling. When you feel happy and fulfilled, you merely create a ripple effect on your loved ones. Kids are sensitive human beings. They sense your energy and level of fulfilment in life from the early stages. Happy mum, happy children. They also sense the opposite.

No Wonder Woman shield

It's easy to fall into the trap of a defeating mindset if you feel your priorities are competing, especially on days when you feel like you can't cope with this balancing act anymore. You are more resourceful than you think. There are times which simply suck. In those hard times, I'm going to ask you to ask for help. Many of us, myself included (especially in the early years), find asking for help to be a painfully excruciating experience. Put your ego aside, your 'shoulds' and high expectations for perfectionism. Acknowledge there's a problem and ask for H E L P. I coached a group of tech mums in Krakow, Poland, and one of them told me that when she was on the edge of having a breakdown, holding a top tech job and with two small children at home, she reached out to her manager and finally spoke up. To her surprise, she got all the support and time she needed to regain energy. She thought she'd be fired. That company is one of the smart leading organisations in 3D printing and augmented reality. They value employees. She was back, and she's delivering results, more resilient than before, and her kids are growing up fine.

Siesta time

This one is for women who are taking the part-time or home-office path. When the kids have downtime, and enjoy siestas or playtime with others, most women would use that time to take care of the home tasks and chores. However, this prime time can be an opportunity for you to re-energise and strategise. Take care of critical tasks; avoid using these golden moments for things that can wait or things you can delegate. In other words, prioritise your important and urgent matters that make a difference to your work.

It takes a whole village to raise a child

A true African proverb. Yes, recognise that you do not have to do it all alone. As a working mum, you can become affiliated to support structures and circles that you can reach out to naturally when you need help. Once you've assessed they are professional, trust them with your childcare. Avoid the over controlling or micromanagement style. If you are getting a nanny or taking your child to a day-care, have a mantra that helps you disconnect as you leave your child. I met Marcela, a Spanish friend who is also a scientist at a food company in Basel, Switzerland. She told me: "The trick here is to work in the office fully focused, as if you don't have a child, and when you are at home enjoy the time being a mum as if you don't have a job." Focused mindfulness.

Get rid of your naysayers

You don't need critics and people who aren't on board with your vision. I used to struggle with this one since critics are sometimes subtle and they can get under your skin if you let them.

Patricia, a researcher at one of the labs in Basel, was about to be promoted to a well-earned VP position. In one of our sessions we talked about the irony criticism that she's had from stay-home mums and neighbours who knew she had a 100% job. She described awkward moments at her kids' school events, feeling like a surprise guest at a dinner party – unexpected. Comments such as: *"Long time no see… Are you on holiday?... What a surprise to see you around, you are always travelling… Did you bake that yourself or just bought it at the bakery on the corner, I bet you don't have time?"* while adding a little sarcastic smile. I could tell those comments bothered her. I could relate somehow. A few years ago, when my coaching practice grew exponentially, I used to let those critics get under my skin too. No more. Over the years, I learned not to take such comments personally. No one knows what balancing acts we do in our families to have a fulfilling life.

Here are a few tips: don't hang out with people who are quick to criticise you or compare your role as a parent. Pretend you don't hear those comments, unhook yourself from those conversations. You can do it. Don't even waste time feeling guilty about not stopping by for a 'quick chat' with those people and gracefully leave. Nurture your time with like-minded people. They may or may not be other mums.

Put on your oxygen mask first

Last year on my way to Cabo Verde to empower African women, the flight attendant's security announcement reminded me of this strategy. It said: "If there is a drop in cabin pressure, oxygen masks will automatically be released. Pull the mask and adjust it. Secure your mask before assisting others." What!? As a parent, my first reaction would be to assist my children first, though in life, just like on a plane, this step is critical.

There's a need for working mums to reclaim themselves. You are giving so much to everyone, taking care of so many people and other matters, that it's easy to forget about your own needs. As you get exhausted or overtired, you need to acknowledge you need time for yourself. Establishing healthy boundaries around self-care and recognising your individual needs is wearing your oxygen mask. Self-care, rest, sleep time, whatever the heck fills up your cup, something fun, and 'me-time' are in that oxygen mask. It can be as simple as taking a walk, coffee with friends, being alone, exercise, meditation, giving yourself little breaks, reading a good book and retaking up some of your past hobbies.

The monster: guilt

Guilt is perhaps the most useless emotion there is. It doesn't help us at all, zero, nada. It's a monster that makes a working mum feel that their career may be damaging their kids' future.

Sheryl Sandberg, COO of Facebook, suggested a quote that resonated with me about ditching guilt, and it is hanging on my office window: "Go for progress, not perfection." Release the tension of being a perfect mum, trust the resilience of your kids and trust that everything has a solution. When you let go the super high (and unnecessary) standards of being a mother, it's a relief and an empowering strategy. *Hasta la vista*, guilt! Trust me, others will sort things out for themselves too; you don't need to fix absolutely everything for everyone.

Tell them why and they get on board

Once the kids are old enough to understand more of what you do, it's key to let them know *why* you do it. When you can articulate it easily according to their age, you'll be surprised how it can increase their support and understanding. The same applies to people around you who you want on board as part of the village. My friend Priska, a medical doctor and head of the paediatric unit in a Swiss hospital, explained to her eight-year-old what she does, and he's excited about hearing her stories and what she does as a doctor when she's back from her job. He's aware of her mission and why it's essential. Her neighbours, who she communicated her 'why' to, are also pitching in when she needs them, and she no longer feels apologetic about asking for help.

Your spouse is a partner, not a babysitter

My same friend, Priska, tells me her extended family thinks her husband babysat their son when she was at work. Men who take care of their kids are not babysitting, they are parenting. You can also help in this process. Being too controlling, possessive or critical on the way he does things when you are gone will be disempowering and not a good thing. I often think that whoever is at home with the kids is the CEO and gets to run the show. The other parent can come home and show support.

Yahoo CEO, Marissa Mayer, has been scrutinised about being a mum of three kids and her job as CEO. She talks about how she needs quality time with her kids while at the same time wanting to have an impact and loving her work. As simple as that. Her background in artificial intelligence has created an impact on the company, and at the same time it was important to keep going throughout her pregnancies. So come up with a blend of working styles that help you prioritise and acknowledge what matters to you. A similar answer came from Alibaba CEO, Mike Evans, father of nine kids, pointing out it's about having support in his family. Except that men are less likely to be asked: *"How do you do it all?"*

The most important career decision?

For women in STEM the following statement may shock you. I was shocked when I first read it. Then I gave it more thought. Sheryl Sandberg's quote reads: "The most important career decision you'll make is who you'll marry." OK, this is if you decide to marry. However, after giving it thought I'll have to agree. Depending on his and your expectations on how the important priorities get aligned in life – things like earnings, childcare, homemaking –

roles are things that depend on the aspirations and expectations of two people.

Having the critical conversation before having a baby is vital. Parenthood will put this aspect to the test. Getting organised, making choices about who gets to cancel attending a meeting when the child is sick, or who gets to cancel a work trip if there's something important at home going on, who will accept a promotion or commute, all those are choices that depend on who you choose in life and his goals, dreams, priorities and understanding. By the way, priorities change in each phase, updating this alignment is an ongoing effort. Have you had those important talks with your partner? It's almost never too early to have these big 'A' agenda talks.

Know your priorities

There's no way to be a perfect mother, but a million ways to be a good one. Let's be honest here – something's got to give. Susan Wojcicki, CEO of YouTube, had her fifth child and admitted she leaves the office by 6pm. When asked about being a mum and the head of YouTube (now what could be a $70 billion standalone company), she acknowledged that distinguishing and establishing priorities are part of her success. In other words, being clear about what matters is the key, both at home and at work. She often says how being a mother has made her more productive, having more focus on growth and potential. Define what matters, what gives you results and impact, it's not essential to pick up all the 'balls'. In fact, letting some balls drop is one of the best strategies to getting things done. It's a paradox, though: when you define what works for you and your family, and release yourself from the burden of external critics and expectations, magic happens.

On an international TV interview, Mary Barra, General Motors CEO, was asked if it was possible for her to run a major automaker and be a good parent at the same time. I was pleased to see how she paused, smiled slightly – if she was upset about the question I didn't notice it – she said: "You know, I think I can. I have a great team; we're on the right path… I have a wonderful family, a supportive husband and I'm pretty proud of the way my kids are supporting me in this." I wonder if the male presenter had ever asked the question to a male CEO: "Can you be a good dad while you are the CEO of XYZ company?" I wonder what he would have answered.

Happy hour

This hack isn't about the cocktail happy hour you might enjoy when you feel overwhelmed – even though that can help. Happy hour or 'special time' is a strategy that Natasha, a Mexican physicist and one of my closest friends, shared with me. When you are at home, blocking a 'precious time' on a regular basis with your child is golden. It's not enough to hang out at home, supervise tasks or chores, or even meals. Special time is when you can consciously decide to be in 'flight mode', disconnected from the rest of the world, and your child gets to choose an activity, game, topic or a chance to connect. Interestingly it doesn't require long periods; this connection, when it's done well and regularly, can be 15 or 20 minutes long, though it's rewarding for both.

I am still working, at times, on not feeling guilty if I have long trips in my calendar. I quickly remind myself of the benefits we are all enjoying because as a working mum I get to do what I do. I suggest next time you feel you need that oxygen mask, or you want to ditch guilt or are faced with old-fashioned mum-questions, I want you to remember these great compelling reasons to keep working after you have kids:

• Financial independence

• You can potentially secure future earnings

- Gain personal fulfilment

- You will raise strong, healthy kids with a positive role model in life

- You will be happier, and it has a ripple effect on your loved ones

- And ultimately, you can continue to have a positive impact on science or tech, engineering, business and/or mathematics! And that, my friend, is something the world needs.

I suggest ditching the term 'work-life balance'. In this new era, work and life are not disconnected areas, and it's an outdated idea between the two choices in perfect equilibrium. Instead I suggest to consider w*ork and life integration or harmony*. Think of it as arrangement of congruity. And it's a personal equation. Nobody can tell you how your week should be or look like, or how these two elements should blend. Though listening to your intuition, being clear about your life/career purpose and setting healthy boundaries for yourself are essential.

If you decide motherhood is for you, you can be a good mum and also follow your dreams.

Key points Chapter 13

- You can pursue your professional dreams and goals while you are a mother, if that's what you really want. Yes, you can.

- Compelling research indicates that children who grow up with working mothers learn invaluable life skills from them (independence, strong work ethic, resilience and great role modelling). Women brought up by working mothers are more likely to achieve supervisory roles in future jobs, and also to earn higher incomes for the family. Men brought up by working mothers are more likely to support gender equality, take care of household chores and also spend more time taking care of the family as adults.

- Just like on an airplane, you'll have to put on your oxygen mask first before helping others. Meaning, as a smart STEM mum, if you want sustainable results, make sure you don't run out of energy and prioritise your wellbeing, you'll be able to look after the others in a better way.

- This chapter explored why guilt, although it's a useless emotion, can affect career decision-making for working mums. Being a successful STEM working mum will also require you to accept and ask for help when needed, develop a support network of care givers who you trust. Get rid of the naysayers and critics. After all, only you'll know what sort of life/work integration you'll need.

14.

ADVANCED STRATEGIES FOR WOMEN IN POWER AND ON BOARDS

"Being the first female CEO of one of the Big Four, I certainly intend to pay it forward."

CATHY ENGELBERT, CEO DELOITTE AND CHAIR OF BOARD
OF DIRECTORS CATALYST

If you are the person who is in charge and invests and grows a company, it's good to know that your customers are already rapidly powering up their business using digital solutions and technology. I bet you and your organisation want to do everything possible not to be left behind.

The World Economic Forum predicts that by 2030 women can, and will, be critical in leveraging this revolution to benefit our global society. We can all play a role here.

Leading companies, businesses like yours, are launching efforts with growing urgency. You see, investing in STEM fields within your organisation is much more than a do-gooder mission. A company whose employees are representatives of their customer base serves its shareholders better.

We know there is tremendous competition for talent. What would you have to do to expand the potential of your workforce and be future ready?

Out of the top Fortune 500 companies, those with three or more female directors see a return on investment capital increase of at least 66%, a return on equity increase by at least 53% and a return on sales increased by 42%. Not bad for investing in attaining equality. It's clear if you want to improve the financial performance of your organisation, increasing innovation is a must. Diverse teams that work well outperform the competition, every time.

If the staff turnover rate is a headache for your company, the solution could be diverse teams (including more women) and this can result in a lower turnover rate of up to 22% (according to Gallup finding). If you are having trouble finding good hires, it turns out that cultures that are more inclusive also have an easier time with recruiting.

Do you need more evidence to help you consider increasing the number of women in your science or math department? Women's talent and voices are essential to problem solving and innovation at the heart of engineering, math, physics or biotechnology challenges. We know that a lack of women in these areas didn't originate in the corporate world or in a company like yours, or even within your industry. This problem has existed for decades. One of the origin points is the false notion that girls aren't good at math and science.

So, here are some concrete ideas and success stories. I encourage you to be action driven and see which action(s) you and your organisation can help implement. Remember, every idea you help implement can impact your bottom line and get you better business results. As simple as that.

Role modelling

If you see it, you can be it. When someone like Susan Wojcicki, YouTube CEO, mother and thought leader gets featured, she inspires young Millennials to go into, and stay in, the tech world. Portrayals of women scientists and engineers in the media have begun to change. The incredible success story of the African-American women working at Nasa in the 1960s is featured in the film *Hidden Figures*, and has had an impact. Their work in engineering and mathematics helped put the first humans into space, this example inspires girls, and young female scientists can see themselves as active decision-makers and creators, not simply followers in secondary roles in science.

Actions you can take

Review your company website. Your company's marketing campaigns and ads. Even places within your office environments. What do you see? Pictures and slogans created by and for a particular group of professionals alone? Mostly male engineers or men in suits, male decision-makers teaching or achieving?

Do a systematic review. Take note, ask for help from others. We tend to see and hear what we want to see and hear. We are all biased, so carry out these actions with the support of a diverse team. You'll be able to pick up on the messages that women within your organisation and potential hires are getting when they view your organisation from the outside.

Decision: what needs to change? Is it the message or images, or both? Reflect on your values as a company and who you want to have on your workforce. Expand these thoughts and actions to your HR and Talent & Development departments. Get them on board. Feature gender diversity in executing roles. A picture speaks more than a thousand words.

The high cost of unconscious bias

We are all biased. Even myself. This is my epiphany. A few years ago, after a seminar for women in Kuala Lumpur, Malaysia, a woman approached me to point out that every time I used the word 'leader' I then went on to conjugate all verbs and actions in the masculine form. And I was delivering a diversity and leadership seminar to an audience mostly made up of women! Since then I've trained myself to use expressions that are either gender neutral or I take the time to say she/he leads, his and her team, etc. You get the point. As leaders, we are the ones who first need to look in the mirror and raise self-awareness. Because what we say and do is being watched and mirrored by our people. So, what are you biased about? Gender? Race? Background? Academic credentials? A brave self-reflection exercise can go a long way.

Action to take

Schedule regular opportunities to review unconscious bias in your team and your departments. It's a corporate cultural mind-shift. Effective, unconscious bias training is not a short, half-day investment, it's an ongoing effort that really pays off. It's also important to bring all new hires on board as soon as they get on your boat. It can take time to measure the impact. Inclusion can be tricky to qualify/quantify, gender diversity can be seen in numbers (hiring) though it's the number of promotions you should pay attention to.

Male champions of change

When we know that men run over 95% of the most powerful companies in the world, it's imperative we partner up on this effort. In your company, this means no change will happen if you don't gain their buy-in and reduce resistance amongst your male teams. Male sponsors and mentors are accelerators in this process. This can help equalise opportunities for women in STEM fields, in your organisation, at all levels.

Action to take

Open up your company's website. Go to About Us – or Board of Directors. What do you see? If you are not seeing at least 30% female faces in that picture, your organisation is not only leaving money on the table, it's not setting an example that inspires gender diversity, innovation and equality. This isn't about blame or finger pointing. It's aimed at raising awareness and triggering meaningful actions.

Choose key male ambassadors to help you set a positive tone, and model an open and diverse approach to equality. You are looking for champions. For this step, you'll need to pick some leaders at the highest level of your organisation as well as some at the mid and entry level. Invite them to discuss your thoughts, actively listen to their ideas. Review simple actions you can start taking.

Spot your hot jobs

There are high-level jobs, and then there are the *real* high-level jobs. Those are the kind of positions where you get to shine, have lots of visibility and even gain international attention. Those are critical to your company's success. Within your organisation, who's next on your success plan to occupy those hot-jobs within the next three to six years? Where are the women in that pipeline? Time to take action.

Catalyst (a well-respected global non-profit that helps companies build workplaces that work for women) has proven that whilst women are usually selected based on performance and proven record, men are selected based on potential. It's the devil's cycle for women, isn't it? Even some of the most successful CEOs in the world admit that they weren't ready for their jobs as CEOs when they got them. If they had been selected purely on proven record, they probably wouldn't have got the job. Someone saw what they could potentially do for a company and hired them. Once you are at the top, of course, your performance will continue to speak for you. So, consider selecting women on potential, too.

Action to take

Identify the hot-jobs in your company. Here are a few clues you want to look for: jobs that have mission-critical roles. Those include things like profit and loss responsibility, managing a considerable amount of direct reports, responsibility for overseeing more than one continent, essential budget responsibility, or those requiring international relocations. Establish metrics that can help you determine a good representation of women in mission-critical roles.

Establish current criteria and co-create a new set of rules with a diverse team to give your plans for success more potential. Find out how candidates for the hot-jobs are being recruited or identified in the early stages. Review the criteria to fill those positions and co-create ways to open up those criteria to be inclusive and based on potential, and not simply based on existing proven performance.

Support women in those roles where necessary (high-level sponsorship and mentoring from male and female peers). Give your HR team the skills and resources they will need to track key data and to best inform you when making these strategic decisions.

Re-energise your board of directors: pay attention to how board recruitment policies work. Reach out outside your traditional network of contacts to find diverse candidates so that your board truly reflects the consumers and communities they serve. This is, by the way, the best reason you can give to your shareholders should you face resistance from their side. Trust me.

Know your critical mass

McKinsey studies and the most recent research made available by Catalyst confirm: the 'magic number is 30%' of critical mass. Kind of the 'tipping point' at which things start happening. A concrete example of this is when there is a critical mass of 30% of women on boards, companies outperform on return and equity compared to all-male boards.

Action to take

Simple math. Consider your board composition. What's that 30% number you need to achieve to start gaining more return on equity and sales, and impacting the bottom line? What needs to happen to close the gap?

Once you reach 30% of women on your board, the next steps are easy. I recently talked to the CEO of a global Swedish retail company. She said: "Gabriela, once you get to 30% the rest goes fast and smooth, we no longer talk about quotas or numbers. The continued increment happens." She describes how, when the company got to 30% at board and top management level, corporate sustainability was increased and, interestingly, their stock market value went up along with it. As a consequence, it attracted more women at all levels.

On average, women only apply for a job when they meet 100% of the qualification requirements, while men apply for the same job when they meet only 60%. Surprised to hear this? Several studies from Lean In to Catalyst and internal reports from some of the biggest tech companies reveal similar findings.

While you may be thinking that this comes down to self-confidence, my experience and research indicate there's more to it. Women don't apply for new jobs, and high-profile positions in particular, if they don't have 100% of the qualifications required due to various reasons, one of which is being too respectful of the recruiters' time. They will avoid putting themselves out there if there is a chance of failure and will assume those requirements are actually needed for the job. Men justify applying without 100% of the required qualifications by arguing they are quick learners, they can get up to speed on the job and can compensate for the gap by using other skills. It's interesting, right?

So, if your talent pipeline and recruiting efforts are not flowing with female applicants, you now know more about why this may be.

Lastly, something I'd like you to consider.

Women are leaving STEM jobs in droves. We know they leave the STEM pipeline in large numbers due to several reasons. One of these is the 'baby penalty'; one in two mothers in STEM fields report experiencing discrimination in the workplace related to parental leave or return after having a baby at some point. Women working in STEM fields are more likely to experience hostile work environments than in other areas. Other reasons are pay-gap and lack of recognition, sorts of discrimination and more.

Action to take

Get familiar with the company's level of inclusion or hostility, if it exists. Navigate through each level of your organisation and observe. Encourage an open-minded environment. A genuine place for people to be themselves. As a leader, you always have a choice on how you'll speak, how to express your view, on the quality of the questions you ask. Your views about failure and making mistakes will determine how much creativity and exploration you will have in your organisation. If you use gender expressions to articulate concepts associated with leadership, strength, power, strategy, then your people will immediately associate those with whatever language you are using. Finally, if you want to remove toxicity and hostility that may make talent vanish, you are the best example to start doing the right thing. Choose courage and ethical leadership over comfort.

If you are to enhance the power of women in STEM fields in your company, the time is now. If you want to get something you and your company haven't got yet, you need to be ready to do things you've never done before. Go for it!

Bringing it all together

An example of this is one of the largest food companies in the world, based in Germany. The leadership team wanted to tackle the lack of female talent in their pipeline and, moreover, how it was hurting their business. They launched three ideas to raise diversity and their profitability grew like fruit on trees! A mentoring programme that built bridges between women and leadership, from mid-management to their C-suite level. They boosted diversity and injected a good sense of true inclusion. Their pipeline for hot-jobs comprises at least 50% women who, in the next three years, will reach the highest leadership levels within their company. Their top male managers are often speakers on diversity panels where the topic of gender diversity is discussed. This sends a message that says it is something they care about and they walk the talk.

One of the groundbreaking companies in packaging and distribution started a Diversity & Inclusion (DI) programme within their engineering department. The ambitious mission was not only to bring more women into engineering and design, but also to increase different ethnicities. They implemented a series of small changes, which had a big impact that shifted the company culture. As a result, they now report seeing a 75% increase in the number of women at executive level, a 65% increase in women directors, and a 30% increase in mid-level women managers. The loyalty of their customers and share value increased too. Their programmes were globally led and locally driven. Their CEO told me that they often call for 'Organisational self-reflection days' – days in which their employees are encouraged to reflect, find empathy for others and discuss unconscious bias. They got it. It's a continuous effort, business imperative and not only an HR programme.

Key points Chapter 14

- If you are the person who is in charge and grows a company, runs a lab, leads in academia or similar STEM fields, you are in an excellent position to power up the 4th Industrial Revolution with diversity at the core.

- This chapter explored the different ways and best practices to remove obstacles, support the advancement of women in your organisation from staffing, recruiting, to promoting. The World Economic Forum predicts that by 2030 women can, and will, be critical in leveraging this revolution and benefit society as a whole. We can all play a role here.

- Bringing men into this conversation and convincing them to take action is part of the job at this level.

- Know that the critical mass, where true transformation starts, is 30 % of women in representation.

- Some of those important hurdles that prevent women advancing are unconscious or implicit biases against what it means to be or have women in powerful decision-making positions. This obstacle alone is costly. It affects your talent pipeline and increases staff turnover. Leaders like you are the front of the pack and can be change agents. It is a team effort; you cannot do it alone, therefore gaining support from all parties involved is key.

Conclusions

Today something incredible will happen. A female engineer somewhere will finally speak up during a meeting and will put her new ideas out there. Not without fear, but in spite of it. A scientist in a lab will request and get the grant she needs for her groundbreaking research. A smart woman in technology will pitch her idea to a steering committee to gain funding and nail it! A female team of a startup in artificial intelligence will present their company to venture capitalists and get the investment they need. A professional in cybersecurity will speak up during a conference call courageously, disagree on bad practices, and demand better governance.

A young woman will follow her heart and enrol in the first course on her path to study astrophysics instead of following a traditional path that society wished for her. A female software developer will launch her first product, she's afraid of failing though that won't stop her from trying. Somewhere a working mother will leave her kid at the daycare for the first time knowing her kid will be fine, while she goes to her STEM job and changes the world. All of them know that doing nothing is worse than taking these risks. Their ideas and contribution are too important for our future to let them rest in silence.

In the course of the years I've been a coach, empowering women in hundreds of organisations, I've heard success stories from all over the world. These techniques, tools and strategies do work. I know many of them may seem simple at first, though as I mentioned before, they are not necessarily easy to put into practice.

Let's recap. You've heard about the current situation of women in STEM and why it's imperative to accelerate change. Therefore, we've covered tactics and strategies that can serve you to navigate and successfully thrive as a powerful smart woman in STEM fields.

Now you know you are in more control than you probably thought you ever were.

You've got a personal life/work compass that can light up priorities and values as you continue to make courageous decisions in your field. You know how your mindset and behaviours can power up your results, they are not entirely determined by your context or other people. You are now ready to tackle fears and take action.

You've got better tools to negotiate. Remember you don't get what you deserve, you get what you negotiate. You've got tips and tricks to come across as the valuable, competent and approachable professional you are. You've got *magic glasses,* the kind of glasses that help you detect good and bad bosses a mile away, how to better work with them and still get what you want. How to support other women and why it's crucial. We women are the ones who can power up this cohesion and collective growth. Together, we are stronger.

Women in powerful positions have got a good set of ideas and best practices to implement and advocate for change in the 4th Industrial Revolution. If you are a STEM mum, you have got a new Swiss Army knife of tools version 4.0 to help you thrive in this exciting and intense phase of life.

You now know how to bring men into this conversation and the important role they've got to play as we all move forward in this rapidly changing world of technology and advancement. Let's not forget to keep humanity at the centre of new developments. Diverse teams perform better. Gender parity is a business imperative for organisations.

My friend, when you decide to put these tactics into action and choose your battles wisely, your life and work will unfold in ways you can only dream of. Be wise and choose the right tool for the right time, know what really matters to you and don't sweat the small stuff. Don't be too hard on yourself, have empathy for you, do the best you can and move on. You'll either succeed or survive. Be strategic, respond without reacting. The power lies on the short period between what happens and what you decide to do about it.

Last story. The decision to write this book, although as I said started years ago, came on an early morning hour of December last year with strong determination. I had a terrible dream. In my nightmare, the doctor had given me some bad news about my health, and as I heard the news I immediately felt *one* regret in my dream. I woke up in a cold sweat. My husband, Daniel, woke up too. I told him all about it and that the *first and only regret* in my dream was not to have written this book for *you*. So, here it is. I am hoping though, I still have many years to live. I want to continue rocking the boat and making waves, challenging the status quo wherever I go because I'm never it. After all, growth and great things never came from comfort zones and status quos.

For you, I wish you never stop being the smart and courageous woman in the room who dares to say no to obsolete practices, bad leadership, to complacency or to the ordinary. I wish you leave nothing that is important to you unsaid or undone.

As a smart woman in science, technology, engineering and mathematics, the world is counting on you. I am counting on you. I wish you risk going too far, so you can find out how far you can go. You don't need to save the world in the 4th Industrial Revolution, though you do need to *make a difference*.

You've got this, smart woman. Go!

Notes and references

Before you read this book

The Global Gender Gap Report, 2017. Schwab K., Zahid S., Ratcheva V., 2017. Switzerland, World Economic Forum.

Gapminder, 2018. Prof. H. Rosling, O. & A. Rosling, Independent Swedish Foundation.

The Fourth Industrial Revolution, Prof. K. Schwab, 2017. Crown Business Publishing.

WES Statistics, Women's Engineering Society, Dr. S. Peers, January 2018.

Stemming the Tide, Why women leave engineering. N. A. Fouad PhD, R. Singh PhD, M. E. Fitzpatrick PhD, Jane P. Liu PhD.

Why Are There So Few Women Mathematicians? Topaz and Sen. Prof. Macalester College.

Women are underrepresented on the editorial boards of journals. Emilio M. Bruna, Alyssa H. Cho, 2016.

The Tech World Is Still a Man's World. Felix Richter, March 8, 2018, and August 7, 2017, Clare Byrne, Formative Content Davos, WEF 2017.

The Culture of Inclusion Journey Knowledge Center. Crunch base study on female founder representation of US-based companies was published in May 2015, revised 2017, G. Teare, April 19, 2017.

Chapter 1

The Future of Jobs. World Economic Forum, January 2016.

Jobs lost, jobs gained: What the future of work will mean for jobs. J. Manyika, P. Batra.

Technology and the Future of Work. A. Peralta, A. Roitman, International Monetary Fund Insights Analysis, 2018.

Chapter 2

A Theory of Human Motivation, Maslow, 1943 paper.

Neuroscience and Human Motivation. J. Reeve, W. Lee. The Oxford Handbook of Human Motivation, 2012.

The Happiness Advantage, S. Achor, 2010.

Chapter 3

Effect of Stereotype Activation on STEM Women's Career Narratives. Mary Jean Amon, University of Cincinnati's psychology program. Washington DC, 2014.

M&M Convince Matrix created by BA Coach Gabriela Mueller Mendoza, Berne, Switzerland.

Robert Cialdini, considered the leading social scientist in the field of influence, Regents' Professor Emeritus of Psychology and Marketing at Arizona State University, author of *Influence*.

How to Tell a Great Story, C. O'Hara, Managing yourself, HBR, 2014.

DEEP, Persuasion and Influence, Harvard Business Review, 2010/ revised 2017.

Research on Gravitas and Executive Presence by Center for Talent Innovation, organization in New York.

Chapter 4

Eurostarts Statistics Explained, a guide to European statistics
https://ec.europa.eu/eurostat

Toastmasters International, non-profit educational organisation
www.toastmasters.org

Executive Presence: The Missing Link between Merit and Success.
Hardcover. S. Hewlett, 2014.

Why Women Stay Out of the Spotlight at Work. P. Fielding-Singh,
D. Magliozzi, Harvard Business Review, 2018.

How to talk so people listen, Julian Treasure, TED Speaker, 2014.

How to sound credible. Dr. L. Sicola, TEDxPenn, 2015.

Chapter 5

Why The 5 Second Rule Works: The Science Explained. Robbins,
M. 2017.

A Bias for Action. Heike Bruch, Sumantra Ghoshal. Harvard
Business School Press, 2004.

Designing the Life You Really Want. Dave Evans, Stanford Life
Design Lab, Stanford eCorner, 2017.

Chapter 6

Why Women Need a Tribe. T. Taljaard, 2016

Why women should do less and network more. Based on a Pew
Survey, quoted by C. Bartz, L. Lambert, 2014.

Chapter 7

Simple ways for women to rethink office politics and wield more influence at work. Kathryn Heath, December 2017.

Polls and Research by B. Cain, I. Hui, Research Bill Lane Center for American West, May 2018.

Research and Observations by Jane Horan, EdD on The Power of Positive Workplace Politics.

Chapter 8

DISC Assessment Validation Study Summary. Calculations performed by D. T. Snider-Lotz PhD.

Everything DiSC, D. Baum, 2017.

Everything DiSC for Leaders Research Report, Inscape Publishing.

Chapter 9

Power and Influence in Organizations. R. M. Kramer, M.A. Neale. Sage Publications, Thousand Oaks, 1998.

The Power of Persuasion. Putting the science of influence to work in fundraising. Robert B. Cialdini, 2003.

The Intent to Persuade Transforms Language via Emotionality. M. Rocklage, Derek Rucker, 2018.

Chapter 10

Women who don't negotiate their salaries might have a good reason. Harvard Business Review. C. Exley, M. Niederle, L. Vesterlund, HBR, April 12, 2016.

Learn how to defuse the anchoring bias and make smart first offers. The Program on Negotiation at Harvard Law School. K. Shonk, 2018.

The Frequency of 'Brilliant' and 'Genius' in Teaching Evaluations. D. Storage, Zachary Horne, A. Cimpian, Sarah-Jane Leslie, 2016. The Brilliance Effect.

Gender Bias Against Women of Color in Science Double Jeopardy? Joan C. Williams, Katherine W. Phillips & Erika V. Hal. University of California, 2014.

Chapter 11

Lean In Org is an initiative of the Sheryl Sandberg & Dave Goldberg Family Foundation, it aims at empowering women. Based in USA.

Disrupt Bias, Drive Value: A New Path Toward Diverse, Engaged and Fulfilled Talent. S. Hewlett. R. Rashid Center for Talent Innovation, 2017.

Chapter 12

A Gallup, an American research-based, global performance-management consulting company. Founded by George Gallup in 1935. This poll refers to research of more than 1 million employed US workers, 2017.

The Queen Bee and The King Wasp: What's All The Buzz? Catalyst. M. Chamberlain. August 24, 2017.

Workplace bullying: a complex problem in contemporary organizations. Georgakopoulos A., Wilkin L., Kent B. (2011). International Journal Business Social Science.

Chapter 13

Ikigai (pronounced 'eye-ka-guy') is, above all else, a lifestyle that strives to balance the spiritual with the practical. Japanese term that translates to 'reason for being'.

Family and Changing Gender Roles IV. ISSP, Family and Changing Gender Roles ISSP 2012. No. 5900.

Mounting Evidence of Advantages for Children of Working Mothers Upshot. C. Miller, New York Times, 2015.

Chapter 14

Why Gender Diversity is Integral to your Company's Success. 2017, Vercida.

Why women don't apply for jobs unless they are 100% qualified. T. Sophia Mohr, HBR, 2014.

Lean In: Women, Work and the Will to Lead. S. Sandberg, August 2015.

What Exactly Constitutes a 'Critical Mass'? Gender Diversity in the Boardroom and Firm Performance. J. Joecks, K. Pull, K. Vetter, University of Tuebingen. Study mentioned by McKinsey School of Business and Economics Social Sciences Research Network, Working Paper Series (February 22, 2012).

About the author

Energetic empowering coach and professional speaker Gabriela Mueller Mendoza offers strategies for women in STEM to get better results, more often and with less trouble. Her work has a Latin-Swiss flavour and helps women reach decision-making positions worldwide. Her tools are as effective and practical as a Swiss Army knife 4.0.

Her humorous style is direct, bold and spicy. Gabriela is an entrepreneur, mother, catalyst, v-blogger, and philanthropist. Gabriela's work reaches over 80 countries, helps thousands of women in tech giants, engineering corporations, academia, NGOs. Her motto: "Empowering women is the fastest way to positively impact the world."

She worked 12 years for blue-chip companies as a technology specialist. She holds an MBA in Leadership Diversity, and a BA in Information Technology. Her work is practical, based on research and professional expertise. She is originally from Mexico City, but has lived in Switzerland for 20 years with her family.

Read this, thrive, enjoy the ride and get results.

Notes

....

....

....

....

....

....

....

....

....

....

....

....

....

....

....

Notes

....

....

....

....

....

....

....

....

....

....

....

....

....

....

....

Notes

....

....

....

....

....

....

....

....

....

....

....

....

....

....

Notes

....

....

....

....

....

....

....

....

....

....

....

....

....

....

Notes

....

....

....

....

....

....

....

....

....

....

....

....

....

....